The "Good" Student Trap:

Strategies to Launch Your Real Life In College

by Adele Scheele, Ph.D.

Simon & Schuster

Published by
Kaplan Educational Centers and Simon & Schuster
1230 Avenue of the Americas
New York, New York 10020

Special thanks to Laura Barnes, Evelyn Lontok, Linda Volpano, and David Wertheimer.

Editor: Donna Ratajczak
Text Design: gumption design
Production Coordinator: Gerard Capistrano
Production Editor: Maude Spekes
Managing Editor: Kiernan McGuire
Assistant Managing Editor: Brent Gallenberger
Executive Editor: Del Franz

Manufactured in the United States of America
Published Simultaneously in Canada

August 1997
10 9 8 7 6 5 4 3 2 1

Library of Congress Cataloging-in-Publication Data

     Scheele, Adele M.
     The "good" student trap: strategies to launch your real life in college/by Adele Scheele.
     p. cm.
     Includes bibliographical references (p.   ).
     ISBN 0-684-84169-X
     1. Vocational guidance. 2. College students—Employment.
     3. College student orientation. 4. School-to-work transition.
     I. Title.
     HF5381.S343 1997
     650.14—dc21   97-15766
                                    CIP

ISBN: 0-684-84169-X

Contents

Chapter One: **Introduction to College and Career Strategies**   **1**

Chapter Two: **Beating the "Good" Student Trap**   **11**

Chapter Three: **Your "Double Agenda" for Papers and Projects**   **23**

Chapter Four: **Turning Your Professors into Mentors**   **41**

Chapter Five: **The "Hidden Curriculum" of Clubs and Activities**   **53**

Chapter Six: **Real-World Experiments: Internships, Work, Service Learning, and Volunteering**   **71**

Chapter Seven: **Discovering Who You Are and What You Want to Do**   **91**

Chapter Eight: **Finding Your First Job**   **107**

Chapter Nine: **Making the Transition**   **123**

Chapter Ten: **Strategy Checklists**   **129**

Appendix: **Resources**   **137**

This book is dedicated to The Career Center staff and the students of California State University at Northridge.

About the Author

Adele Scheele, Ph.D., an internationally recognized career strategist and consultant on change management, is the Director of the Career Center at California State University at Northridge. She addresses colleges and universities, corporations, and professional associations. Dr. Scheele coaches individuals to discover their callings, resolve their career dilemmas, and realize their goals.

Adele Scheele has also written the best selling *Skills for Success*, and *Making College Pay Off* (Ballantine), and *Career Strategies for the Working Woman* (Fireside/Simon & Schuster). She appears frequently as a career expert commentator on NBC's *Today*, and in other media. She earned a Ph.D. from U.C.L.A. as a Change Management Fellow, a master's degree in English from California State University at Northridge, and a bachelor's degree from the University of Pennsylvania.

Acknowledgments

My heartfelt thanks to Jay Johnson, Del Franz, Ned Jacobs, and Donna Ratajczak at Kaplan; Maureen McMahon at Simon & Schuster; James Stofan at the University of California at Irvine; and to my great staff at Cal State Northridge's Career Center for their many contributions.

—Adele Scheele

Chapter One
Introduction to College and Career Strategies

I have never let my schooling interfere with my education.
—Mark Twain

What do you need to succeed in life? A few lucky breaks won't hurt, but you can't count on them. Today, success in life means learning to grow with ingenuity, and expand with experimentation. Today change means life and becomes the norm, while stability is the anomaly. This is good news because you can learn to identify talents and develop skills and establish consequential relationships that lead to success. Today, achievers in every field learn to trust themselves to find creative projects and collaborate with others. Why not learn about succeeding while you are in life's safest laboratory—college! And like everything else in life, the way we think about college is shaped by the way we value ourselves. We cannot educate ourselves without transforming our self-image. We start with ourselves—our dreams and our fears—and we learn to grow in intellect and courage. Today!

There are many ways to create rich opportunities while you are in college or graduate school. The rule: Don't just fulfill requirements. Instead, turn college into your own personal laboratory. In this laboratory you'll find professors and mentors, creative projects and research programs, and friends for life. No matter how young or old, naive or experienced you are, college is a vital passage to adulthood. It leads from theory learning to practice taking to the discovery of the mind-heart connection. It's up to you to create strategies for realizing the work that can bring you happiness, value, and connection to define your world.

As part of this rite of passage, consider college from a broader perspective. Don't get stuck thinking of college as a stint in the ivory tower, from which you'll descend, four or more years later, into a structured reality where your place is known and your progress assured. It's just not so. You have to learn the most basic skill of all—how to create your place and your path. Why not learn to do that in college?

Essentially, college is a place to experiment with ideas, connect to people, and begin your career. Far from being antithetical to the real world, it's a microcosm of the real world. Everything that you want or need from the real world is there for you in college. Only your fear of limitation of your own talents or abilities or your disbelief in the program's power to deliver can stop you from making this passage through higher education a transformational one for you.

CHANGE 101

Splitting school off from the real world is part of a centuries-old tradition or concept that delineated areas and groups into neat, manageable packages. The twenty-first century, however, has a different, more integrated and accessible vision. But changing structures and desires doesn't happen all at once; a revolutionary transition in how we live and work has been in process over the past twenty-five years.

Boundaries and disciplines, once more rigid, have been loosened and transformed; some have actually merged together, some have disappeared, and some have just been created. The most profound new and overriding change is our coming to terms with the idea that there is no one right answer, no one right way. We seem to be in agreement that there are, instead, many appropriate ways. And those ways are considered and decided in shorter time frames than ever. The ways we think to live—our family and work structures—are our inventions. They can be changed to fit our new definitions and needs.

Starting from the 1970s, I have been coaching people trying hard to find their career direction or to advance within their organizations or own their own. Their dilemmas have ranged from their needs to find new chances, better bosses, experienced mentors, improved skills, worthy missions. As a career strategist, I found myself helping people deal with the complex changes they were experiencing not only in the marketplace, but also in themselves. These difficult dilemmas were all resolvable with planning that incorporated people's real intentions and desires.

Then in 1996, I moved to an academic setting to become the director of The Career Center for Cal State Northridge. I've had the chance to take my own advice, practice what I preach, and apply my understanding of the business world to meet the yearnings and ambitions of students. Whenever I could, I've tried to bridge the gap between academia and the business world through conferences, hands-on internships, and business-faculty collaborations. The process has been amazing for me; I'd like to share what I've been finding.

Work in the '90s, Part One: Chaos

It's hard to describe how fast our world as we know it has changed. It used to be knowable, learnable, because it was fixed in place. Everyone knew what to do, what was expected, and how to change and succeed. But radical changes came fast, breaking down monolithic structures and blurring what was known. Four major factors brought about radical changes in the workplace of the '90s:

- Computers revolutionizing information access
- Organizational restructuring of a rigid hierarchical structure
- New corporate constellations reorganizing through mergers and acquisitions
- Global competition and new alliances

Organizations have reformatted themselves, changing their shapes and their ways of doing business. One-third of the organizations in the Fortune 500 in 1970 had vanished by 1985. Many of the surviving companies have reinvented themselves, practically beyond recognition, as they shift from an old predictable structure to a new paradigm. The old structure was a pyramid with a set hierarchy, with orders and incremental plans issuing top down to the obedient masses of employees, neatly stacked in levels below. The change seemed sudden, a series of forces like a combination of an earthquake and a tornado, flattening these man-made, unnatural, outsized triangles into a more organic spiderweb of activities. Uncharacteristic financial maneuverings split apart or added businesses, bringing together diverse people and structures.

The changes and upheavals in the world of business are mirrored everywhere—including in families and in colleges. Think of diagramming a sociogram of the American family. Unhinged through divorces and reknit through remarriages, we've experienced the anxiety and awkwardness of not knowing how to relate to these newly forged relationships, new and convoluted constellations of stepparents, stepbrothers and sisters, and stepgrandparents, not to mention aunts, uncles, cousins and letting go of those who lived with us.

Just so, business changes discharged millions of workers who thought they knew their jobs and their places. Suddenly even the safest, most secure groups of all—middle managers and clerical staff—were embarrassingly out on the street, scrambling for the unemployment lines, reading classified ads searching for jobs that no longer existed. They were mystified and mad. You might have lived through this yourself; maybe this was a factor motivating you to return to college. Or maybe you witnessed your parents or older sibling caught up in work-caused anxiety.

Hardly any one was spared. Whole departments and divisions were fired, let go, downsized, or, as it is euphemistically called, *rightsized.* The disorder spread like a virus. In nearly every industry, people had to deal with new bosses, sometimes every three or four months. That meant that many had no chance of retiring naturally, after a long term of service, but were abruptly and shockingly fired.

Managers who continued to build and develop their departments had to live with a new anxiety; the constant possibility that their companies would be gobbled up by bigger, richer companies. This new corporate culture created years of anxiety of two sorts: (1) worries about who would be kept on or cast off (2) the struggle to manage more work with fewer employees. Those who stayed found that they had to produce twice or three times as much as before. The stress of these pressures led to new working arrangements. Some employees telecommuted; and some set up home offices as they shifted from full-time employees to consultant status, hired on a per-project basis.

No-fault divorce was happening every day in business. Those who had lost their jobs, much like those who had lost their spouses, lost their very identities and started searching for more than just work; they were looking for themselves. Everyone was learning the too-high cost of depending on an outside system, whether it was a marriage or a corporation. Everyone was learning the twin skills of self-reliance and team-collaboration, and they were learning them the hard way.

Work in the '90s Part Two: Change and Growth

In the mid- to late '90s, the labor market was turning around from its slump. And the marketplace was not just reviving but exploding into new services, new products, new ways of doing business. More small enterprises were created than had ever before existed. Many of them were founded and operated by women, women who were experimenting with employee leadership and ownership. Employees of small businesses now outnumber the employees of all the Fortune 500 companies.

Similarly, many larger organizations started challenging their own meaning and methods. Mission statements were born, conceived and cultivated by employees. Businesses and people used to know exactly what they were going after. Immediate profits, competition, and efficiency of a standard operation had been the key goals. Now such operations are more customized, offering ephemeral knowledge products. Businesses and people are open to experimenting, to looking around to see what might be a good fit. And those answers often mean going global and forming alliances with former competitors: Kodak™ working with Fuji™, for example. Another trend: Whole industries were morphing, collapsing old boundaries. The entertainment industry, for one, which used to be separated into distinct areas such as television, film, radio, or music, is now virtually boundaryless. It now comprises areas such as computer graphics, merchandise, real estate, theme parks, and banking. Artificial divisions are giving way to more organic formations and alliances—locally, nationally, and globally. Consider Disney Hall in Los Angeles, Mickey on New York's 42nd Street; in fact, think EuroDisney and you get the picture.

The very definition of success has changed from a strict focus on financial rewards. Psychological and spiritual values are now part of the equation when we think about work. People have discovered that they have the power to change direction—to reformat that which they called *work*. More and more, people have been giving up their dependency on organizations. Even though they were scared to death, they were starting again as free agents—consultants, solo owners, and entrepreneurs, either by themselves or as members of small consortia.

Look at another change that has affected the texture of our ordinary lives. We have entered cyberspace. Most of us work on our own computers, talk to each other via E-mail, look up information and join interest groups on the Web. It's hard to imagine life before faxes. We've accepted that change is a fact of life on a technological level. In this same spirit, we need to experience our goals and even specific majors as part of a process rather than as final destinations. You'll feel pressured to formulate concrete plans, but don't get stuck in that mindset. You'll find greater rewards in a more fluid process of exploring, declaring, refining, and exploring some more.

Top Trends That Will Affect Your Education and Your Work

1. There's a good chance you won't work in a field directly related to your major.

Most grads I've observed haven't been working in fields directly related to their majors. That's not bad news; it doesn't even mean that they chose the wrong major. It just means that some of what they studied in school wasn't relevant to finding jobs. A degree in religious studies or philosophy may lead to guru status. A degree in science may lead to sales. A third change of majors may strike home, or not. So, if your major isn't pointing true north of your compass for your life's direction, what is? *The megaskills of critical thinking and writing, and self-presentation.* These skills become your internal passport to the worlds of work.

2. Expect to return to school—more than once.

You will join the throngs of people, at every stage of their careers, going back again and again to college or graduate school for new licenses, certificates, and degrees for new or advanced professional training, which in turn, call for more training.

3. Expect to change jobs and even careers many times.

In fact, many people think of all of life as a university, a learning experience wherein curiosity and experimentation and mastery are critical to what we call life.

Technology's "superhighway" changed the place where people are doing their work. Many people are telecommuting, working from home for their companies. They connect with their companies through E-mail, the Net, and the telephone. Some virtual workers miss the comments of friendly co-workers; others welcome the lack of interruptions. People are starting their own home businesses or consulting services in record numbers.

More than ever before, people have been changing jobs and careers. Some have changed jobs out of necessity—their old jobs were erased, incorporated into others, or increased unbearably. Other people were motivated by a search for greater meaning in their lives. Some wanted, for example, to abandon the fast track to lead simpler and/or more family-oriented lives. They were willing to move to smaller towns to start over, or to recharge their connections in city neighborhoods.

I've witnessed people changing whole careers, not just jobs. And not just once or twice. This kind of change is not a fad; it is and will be a continuous process. *Change means constant modification, even reinvention.* The only question is how can you prepare yourself to learn and thrive in this new world. But you're off to the perfect start. You've decided to go to college as a preparation for— and an important part of—life.

Myth: You Need a Degree From a Prestigious School to Succeed

Before you proceed, let me say what doesn't really matter: where you go to college. Successful people from so many different fields have told me that it matters less *where* you go to college than the amount of positive energy you put into going to college. Sure, going to Harvard or Stanford might help you get a better first job. And, yes, having a Wharton M.B.A. or a Yale law degree gives you a leading edge for your first job with the most prestigious corporations, agencies, or firms.

However, there's no guarantee that your Ivy League degree will keep you there. But, for sure, if you don't *use* college in the ways that I'll show you, then it won't offer you much of anything, no matter where you go. And that's a major waste of time, money, and opportunities. Prestigious labels by themselves won't make you who you want to be or take you where you may dream to go. A college degree is not in itself a launcher: *You* are! So no matter where you're matriculated—small college or large university, private or public, single sex or single focused, you can discover yourself and your talents and turn them into a series of opportunities that will start your future success.

Top Six Skills Employers Want

I've been asking employers what kind of graduates they want to hire. No matter who the employers are, they all say the same thing. Employers in every field want to hire people who possess six important skills. Here's what prospective employers want to know about you.

1. Can you think critically and creatively?
2. Can you work collaboratively and cooperatively?
3. Can you speak and write clearly?

4. Do you have the flexibility to manage an increasingly diverse workforce representing an increasing diversity of clients?

5. Do you possess a broad general education as well as computer skills?

6. Do you have a strong work ethic?

How can students develop these skills? It's not a mystery. But it takes a whole lot more than merely playing the passive role of obedient student. It takes courage to search out the endless opportunities within the academic curriculum and the often hidden cocurriculum in which skills for success in the real world are taught.

As it turns out, succeeding in college is just the same as succeeding in business. There will be opportunities to shine, but you have to recognize them even when they are unlabeled and then act on them. It takes intention and action, that mighty combination of will and deed, no matter where you are or what you do. Chances are always there. Trouble is, we just don't believe it. We still think that some force outside ourselves will make us better. We fantasize that if only we could get into the best college or graduate school and into the best program with the best professors, we'd have it made. But life doesn't *do* us. Breaking this kind of thinking will lead us to more appropriate choices based on our own needs and situations. All it takes is the courage to explore.

Here are three great reasons for your going to college:

1. Learning how to enjoy learning

2. Developing the courage, discipline, and ego to risk linking yourself to compelling ideas and people

3. Discovering study and work that illuminate your life

College is a time for preparing yourself for these explorations and experiments. The skills in this book work in every single college setting, small or large, co-ed or single sex, town or country, Ivy League or technical. And, they are the very same skills that promote career success.

A shift has occurred. The Ultimate Test with the One Right Answer is gone. All of us together gave up taking it. Instead, we are embracing the iffy-ness of experimentation, searching for and taking advantage of opportunities, learning by doing, even failing. Life with no right and wrong answers is less orderly but far more interesting and productive. Let yourself be guided by this philosophy in college. This book will show you how.

Author's Notes

About the "Undergrad-itudes" survey

In 1996, I conducted a survey on Kaplan's Web site to explore people's attitudes about college. I wanted to gather information on issues ranging from how people chose colleges or picked majors, to which extracurricular activities they chose and why. Statistics from this survey, which was called "Your Undergrad-itudes," can be found throughout this book.

About the "Career Qs"

Throughout this book, you'll also find career questions from real students, along with my answers. These questions and answers were adapted from my career column in the student newspaper at Cal State Northridge, *The Sundial.*

About the career stories in this book

Some of the names in the stories in this book have been changed to protect the privacy of the individuals involved.

Education is not filling a bucket but lighting a fire.
—*William Butler Yeats*

College is an experiment in hope. It's also a risky investment of anywhere from $25,000 to $125,000, not to mention at least four years of our lives. Whether it's a matter of graduate or undergraduate school, a two- or an eight-year program, we give up a part of ourselves to go to school. In return for our time and money, we expect a new identity and a ticket to the outside world.

GREAT EXPECTATIONS

We come to college with the unspoken anticipation of all that will be done for us. We expect to be made acceptable, valuable, knowledgeable, and finally professional and employable. By graduation, we presume everything will be dazzlingly clear: We will find our calling, brilliantly catapulting us to a guaranteed successful career. This wish, seldom even conscious, lies deep in our hearts. Yet we believe it will happen.

I've counseled thousands of people who once had faith in this magic. All of them had been keenly disappointed when the expected alchemy never took place. It took them years to discover that such a transformation doesn't just *happen*. You've got to *make* it happen. It's fine to believe in magic, but *you* must be the magician. You are the only one who can turn yourself into what you want to be—even if you don't know what that is. You'll want more for yourself than just achieving a prestigious degree or acing a difficult job interview. You'll want to participate in making your life as artful and fulfilling as you can through learning, creating, belonging, contributing—and loving the whole process.

LEARNING SYSTEM DEPENDENCY

The odd thing about life is that we've been taught so many life-less lessons. We've all been conditioned to wait for things to happen to us instead of making things happen. If you think you have escaped this conditioning, then think again. Most of us learned as early as junior high that we would pass, even excel if we did the work assigned to us by our teachers. We learned to ask whether the test covered all of chapter five or only a part of it, whether the assigned paper should be ten pages long or thirty, whether "extra credit" was two book reports on two books by the same author or two books written in the same period. Remember?

We were learning the Formula.

- Find out what's expected.
- Do it.
- Wait for a response.

And it worked. We always made the grade. Here's what that process means: You took tests and wrote papers, got passing grades, and then were automatically promoted from one year to the next. That is not only in elementary, junior, and senior high school, but even in undergraduate and graduate school. You never had to compete for promotions, write résumés, or rehearse yourself or even know anyone for this promotion. It happened *automatically*. And we got used to it.

Survey Responses: Who Talks to Teachers?

In our "Undergrad-itudes" Internet survey, we asked the question, "What were your expectations about college before you went?" Here's how the respondents answered.

Answer	Number of People
Expected more	99
Expected less	92
Thought the intellectual level would be lower	86
Thought it might be hard to make friends	58
Formed my impression from older siblings	46
Thought it would be like the movies	38

What we were really learning is System Dependency! If you did your work, you'd be taken care of. We experienced it over and over; it's now written in our mind's eye. But nothing like this happens *outside* of school. Still, we remain the same passive *good students* that we were at ten or fourteen or twenty or even at forty-four. The truth is, once learned, system dependency stays with most of us throughout our careers, hurting us badly. We keep reinforcing the same teacher-student dichotomy until it is ingrained. Then we transfer it to the employers and organizations for whom we'll work.

All that changes once you find that studying history or art or anthropology can be so much more than just jumping through hoops. Your academic pursuits can lead to new experiences, contacts, and jobs. But so much disappointment has resulted from misusing college, treating it as school instead of life. It's time to retrain ourselves to approach school in the same positive, productive, active way that the most successful people do. Rather than learning to know the subject matter *in* our heart, we've learned it *by* heart. And that makes all the difference between feeling alive and feeling fraudulent.

College can yield all that you wished for. It will be a time for exploring horizons that you never imagined, a time to discover who you are and what your interests and strengths are. College can be a time for accomplishing goals. It's a time to fall in love with ideas and make life-long friends. If you follow the advice in this book, college can be a time for learning how to develop skills that you will need for the rest of your life and that will serve you far beyond your major or your degree.

Career Qs

Q. My parents demand that I major in something that will guarantee me a job. What is the best major?

A. Choosing a major without considering your own skills and passions is a big mistake. But if you are interested in technology, America's fastest growing industry, know that you are in a boom time. According to the Information Technology Association of America's 1996 workforce study, we aren't even able to fill 90 percent of the available jobs in writing software, operating computers, managing computer networks, not to mention maintenance or sales. To make matters worse for the industry, our majors in math and computer science are considerably falling down in enrollments to support the nearly 200,000 information-technology jobs that are available. And that number does not even include small-sized firms or even government agencies. The report warned, "It's as bad as running out of iron ore in the middle of the Industrial Revolution." Talk to a career counselor to find out how you can make technology work for you.

Can Getting A's Be Bad For You?

> *I try to act as if I make a difference.*
> —William James

As a career strategist, I've coached and interviewed a great variety of people. They were teachers, bankers, artists, entrepreneurs, executives, and free agents who wanted to be or who already were successful at what they do. From mapping their lives, connecting the dots of their innate or found passions, I have discovered that people who are successful in their careers were also successful in school. They cared about what they could do, for the others they joined in the process, and for the significance of their efforts. They saw their work as their identity—far more than just a salary or position.

And, in just the opposite way, those who were stuck or frustrated in their careers were carrying over a negative mindset evident even in their school days. I found that these people were holding themselves back, afraid to become involved in their subjects or with their teachers. Not only were they unaware of their self-sabotage, they thought quite the opposite—that they were in fact being "fair" by waiting to be recognized and directed. They were living out a false sense of being "moral."

I call this mindset the *"Good" Student Trap*. But *good* in this case is defined as only waiting passively for good grades, nothing much else. We strive to do only what's expected, even doing it exceptionally, but we wait and wait and wait—first for our teachers, then our professors, and later for our bosses to grade, direct, praise our work and then promote us automatically up to the next level.

Getting Recognition or Not

Look again at school to see what it teaches implicitly. One professor leads a class of any number of students, all equal in nonpower status They take instruction and assignments from the one, ultimate authority. How then do students get attention and recognition? Achievers learn to get the desired attention by doing good work along with building relationships. The polar opposite, the students who were branded failures, also get attention—through poor behavior, but without any lasting rewards. Most of us, however, are overlooked—and do nothing about it. If you doubt this, think back to your earlier days at school, say, in junior high school, when you were first learning about group and peer pressure.

Remember the lessons in system dependency? They boiled down to this hard-and-fast rule:

If we do our work well enough, we will be taken care of.

But nothing could be further from the truth. If we don't take ourselves seriously, learning what motivates and excites us, becoming apprentices to masters and then masters ourselves of our crafts, then we'll lose our purpose, our identity. School is a process of starting this discovery.

Learning to Stay With the Flock

System dependency is not the only damaging thing we learned in the context of school: We learned our *place*. Think back to the life-shaping lessons we learned in junior high cafeteria. As seventh graders, we couldn't eat with eighth graders; they wouldn't let us. We'd be labeled brain-damaged if we invited our teacher to sit with us. But we didn't sit with all other seventh graders either—just the ones who looked like us, acted like us, and came from families just like ours. We locked everyone else out and were locked out in turn. We learned to think that this was ideal; a mistaken ideal.

Here's an example of how wrong and dangerous an ideal can be. In seventh grade, you wouldn't be caught dead going after the attention of your teachers. You'd be labeled a brownnoser!

So which students were recognized and rewarded by being mentored, given support to go on, and opportunities to explore? The answer may surprise you. Only those engaged students who were active in clubs and activities as well as their class work. The key lies in their creating a learning environment that also included building relationships that regular students didn't know even existed. Yet most of us were falsely lulled into a false self labeled "good" by fulfilling the expected curriculum. The alternative was being "bad" by feeling alienated and losing interest or dropping out.

Seventh Grade, Part Deux?

Why make college a sequel to junior high just with older students and tougher assignments? Instead, reframe it so that it resembles being alive in a responsive world which needs your contribution. The longer you sit waiting for life to choose you, the more you become invisible. The passive *"good student"* attitude blocks you from growing motivated and connected to new ideas and networks of people. Doing only what's asked of you even though you do it perfectly is the grossest misunderstanding of what college is all about!

Fear of Failing and How It Can Ruin You

Right. You do have to get good grades on tests. Colleges demand a decent GPA from high school in the first place as proof you can perform. In this way, high academic standing is a prime indicator to future employers of your ability to perform on the job. Similarly the standard for measuring performance in college is The Test. Yet nobody likes taking exams. They always create anxiety. They are not always fair. They don't seem to measure accurately what you really know about your subject. And we don't often learn or remember anything in the process. But we have to live with them—a lot of them.

So what's the problem? The problem is the danger. The danger lies in thinking about life as a test that we'll pass or fail, one or the other, tested and branded by an Authority. So, we slide into feeling afraid we'll fail even before we do— if we do. Mostly we don't even fail; we're just mortally afraid that we're going to. We get used to labeling ourselves failures even when we're not failing. If we don't do as well as we wish, we don't get a second chance to improve ourselves, or raise our grades. If we do perform well, we think that we got away with something this time. But wait until next time, we think; then they'll find out what frauds we are. We let this fear ruin our lives. And it does. When we're afraid, we lose our curiosity and originality, our spirit and our talent—our life. But there are ways to cut short fear and reclaim yourself.

Once burned, twice shy.

PRACTICE EXPERIMENTING

Think about the creative process of a scientific experiment. You develop your hypothesis and then you test it. If it works, you feel gratified being right and proving your theory. But you haven't actually learned anything because you already knew it; now you can confirm results with others.

But suppose you don't prove what you set out to. At first, you feel terrible. The fact is, you were wrong. But have you failed? Only if you think the *experiment* is a *test*. If you do, then by getting the "wrong answer" you feel terrible having failed. Most people decide to quit then and there. Or you go on—in true experimental fashion—restructuring your hypothesis, reexamining your variables, trying another approach, applying your own educated hunches. Only then do you discover things you didn't know before.

It's like the old adage from generations of collected wisdom: "If at first you don't succeed, try, try again." The old adage still applies, but with an addendum: "If at first you don't succeed, try, try again . . . *another way, each time.*" It's a life-fulfilling philosophy that builds both confidence and skill.

Career Qs

Q. I am worried about not making the right career choice and being stuck in that job for the rest of my life. What can I do?

A. You don't have to ever be stuck if you practice taking risks right now. Successful people achieve not just because they're either smart or lucky, but because they are resourceful and courageous. These two qualities will be in great demand in the twenty-first century, for according to the Department of Labor, you will have as many as five different careers in your lifetime. Thirty-three percent of those new jobs aren't even conceived of yet. What such a statistic means is that you can't prepare for one, single career nor can you stand in line for your career to be handed to you like your college registration is. You've got to prepare for many careers.

Start learning the megaskills you'll need throughout your life, now while you're in college. Start networking with professors and counselors on campus, and with employers through internships and jobs. You'll discover fascinating careers though new tasks to learn. It shouldn't be boring!

Think of college not as a test but as an experiment. You're experimenting to find out what you like to study and what you would like to do with your major.

Don't turn college into the Big Test with many small quizzes along the way. You'll end up merely passing: passing tests, passing time, passing up possibilities for achievement, passing through life—stuck in the good student trap.

Susan's Story: Voulez-Vouz Fries With That?

Let's take a look at someone who fell into the good student trap, and think about how she could have used her education differently.

> Susan was used to A's. She graduated at the top of her college class with a B.A. in French, going to class and studying by day and waiting on tables at night at a local coffee shop. Susan hoped that a job in Paris, the city of her dreams, would be hers after graduation. Near the end of her last semester, Susan mailed out dozens of letters requesting job information, but she got no response. Susan discovered that getting employment overseas with an American company was a plum assignment given as a reward to men or women who were already working in their company. There were two other alternatives open to her—teaching or applying to graduate school—but she didn't want to do either. Depressed, Susan felt that college had been a complete failure, a waste of her time and money.

Susan's major was certainly not wasted: The study of another language and culture does provide a valuable framework. But by not *using* college, Susan did fail to uncover and create valuable opportunities. Just for starters, here are eight things she could have done while she was in college to chart her path to Paris.

- She could have developed a relationship with her French professors who might help her network with potential employers as well as find interesting projects.

- She could have studied the French import business.

- She could have volunteered to work for the French consulate.

- She could have worked as a translator for the mayor's office in her college town.

- She could have worked part time at a French bank.

- She could have waited tables at a French restaurant rather than a coffee shop, connecting herself to a French chef or owner, even French customers or suppliers.

- She could have developed her leadership skills by joining the French club and becoming an officer or inviting French artists, politicians, business people to campus.
- She could have spent her junior year in France, working or volunteering part time for an American company with offices in Paris.

Pursuing these cocurricular activities would have taken time, courage, research, and energy. But any one of them would have paid off for her with more than a job. These explorations would have developed Susan's sense of courage and perhaps ignited some passion for a way to use her talents. It also would have been a lot more fun. Even if Susan's grade point average had dropped a little, the tradeoff would have been building blocks to construct her future—and perhaps a passport to Paris, as well as her heart.

Apply these imaginative ways to enhance what you're required to do and what you've chosen. Be proactive in a place where you've been conditioned to be passive. For example, use test taking or paper writing as activities to stimulate a way to discover your calling so that your dreams have a chance of being fulfilled. Combining your curriculum with life is a great way to create a set of goals toward your self-discovery. Dare to experience college as your own laboratory—not an isolated ivory tower. Make it a source of people, contacts, minds, power, creativity, and opportunity. You'll find that the real possibilities of college can be as open-ended as you are open-minded and willing to take risks. It requires your exploring what is yet unknown to you yet beckoning.

You choose how to use college. It can be either a continuation of fulfilling other people's assignments, a time-out from the real world, or it can be a head start into the real world as you create it and contribute to it. It's what you make it. Decide.

Career Qs

Q. My biggest concern is finding a career that offers job stability, security, and advancement. I want to succeed and prosper in life. How can I make sure that I will achieve all this?

A. You won't like this answer, but life has no real guarantees. Security and success are often at odds with each other. But there are careers to choose that are likely to provide you with what you hope for; insurance, accounting, or computer programming, for example. The field of sales is the path to the highest incomes, but this career path is secure only if you are creative and consistent in serving your clients and learning about your product or service. The most secure though not lucrative positions are teaching or government work, even research; these have their own rewards. Your best bet is to get an internship or part time job to discover where you fit best.

STRATEGIES FOR AVOIDING THE "GOOD" STUDENT TRAP

Here are some ways you can put the ideas in this chapter into practice.

How to Build a Network

The first step is to reframe your way of thinking. Don't be so leery of seeking out and connecting with accomplished people—students, professors, and employers. Remember this is the first step in taking yourself seriously. Give up trying to secure your place in the world only by obediently fulfilling other people's expectations and goals.

The process of learning is twofold. First, you need to find out what other people know. Second, find out where you want to forge ahead and make a contribution.

Think of yourself as both an explorer and a builder. It's the process of discovery. Part of what you have to discover is how to interact with other people.

Here are some things you can do.

Join a study group.

If you can't find a study group meeting regularly, start one. Invite some class-mates to meet over pizza to brainstorm about how to reap the many benefits of collaboration. You will learn ways to:

- Organize and prepare material for your classes; set appropriate deadlines so you won't procrastinate

- Build long-lasting friendships with some of the other students in your study group

Check out and join campus activities that appeal to you.

You can get a list of activities from the student affairs office. Pick the activities that you always wanted to join. Do more than just join. Get involved. And make your involvement an exploration of your abilities. Make yourself visit and sit in on a few meetings and events so you can pick one or two activities from your own preferences and direct experiences. Then volunteer in a role that you haven't tried before.

Investigate your best subjects.

Write papers about the fields that interest you. Talk to your professors. Look in the alumni directory (from the alumni office) to find graduates who are employed in fields that interest you. And go meet them. (More on this point in chapter 3.)

Risk asking questions of your academic advisor, professors and administrators. That's what these people are there for.

Go to their offices and ask:

- How they got started

- Surprises they found along the way

- New trends they recognize

- Advice on your best academic or career bets

Make new friends from class and clubs.

Introduce yourself. Meet for lunch or college events and lectures. Keep building your network. People of every age like to be invited; in fact, they are waiting for your invitation or call. Do it. Persistence is hot; shyness is not.

Chapter Three
Your "Double Agenda" for Papers and Projects

*The real voyage of discovery consists not in seeking new
landscapes, but in having new eyes.*
—Marcel Proust

Talent is what you possess. Genius is what possesses you.
—Malcolm Cowley

In primitive societies, boys were initiated by ferocious trials before assuming their roles as men in the tribe. These tests were not only arduous but life risking; only the brave and strong lived through them. The initiates' courage and motivation mattered as much as their physical prowess.

It looks different, but we have the same concept of rites of passage—a kind of proof positive of readiness, youth and inexperience notwithstanding, for young men and women to take their places in society. Sometimes delayed, (for returning students), and sometimes experienced as life threatening, our modern rites are academic.

We prove ourselves in school by writing papers—from short pieces to theses and dissertations—and taking written and oral examinations. These are the proofs of our ability to survive intellectually. Papers and exams become demonstrations to our professors that we can think, analyze, research, understand, and connect with our heritage, and, it is hoped, contribute fresh and useful ideas. These are the survival rituals by which we assume our places in the world as responsible adults.

Develop Double Vision

Can tests and papers be anything more than hoops that we need to jump through? Does this process really give us any skills we can build on?

What about preparation for later life? Can we ever be free of performing within the framework that's handed to us? Yes. Yes. Yes. If you're smart, you'll make these proofs to profs worth even more to you. Think of it that way. Because tests are mandatory and papers are assigned, you have to produce something anyway. You might as well work toward your own best advantage—establishing your own interests and expertise. Get the most mileage out of your time and effort. Create your own "double agenda!"

WHAT YOU REALLY NEED TO KNOW ABOUT WRITING PAPERS

Short or long, papers present the way in to developing your double agenda. Granted, you have to meet the requirements set by the professor for the course. But you can do so much more: discover and meet your own interests, even passions. Sometimes you already know them or have inklings about them, but for the most part, they are the goal of a hunt for the yet unknown. Life becomes the search for your own treasure—your way of belonging and contributing through your acts, your work.

Your professors present their requirements to you as the first step in this treasure hunt. They will give you a topic or range of topics to choose from and tell you how many pages they expect. Figuring out what you want from an assignment is so much harder to do, especially at first, than just ticking off whatever topic seems easiest. Take some time to match your own curiosities and interests to the list of topics given, or else create your own topic and argue for it. The rationale? A good grade, of course, for one thing. Everyone wants that. But what else? Can you take the time out to think about the best outcomes you could wish for by the end of the course? Can you look beyond the semester's course load and consider what you really hope for from the program you're enrolled in?

The first step is to formulate goals of your own from the agenda at hand. Identifying at least one goal allows you to get an extra boost from what could have been just an obligatory classroom assignment to mine the gold inside you and inside the course's world. Instead of just being the "good" student, you can start "using" school strategically. You'll be taking advantage of the opportunities that college gives you by allowing for scientific, intellectual, and psychological explorations and connecting it to others who make it their living.

Writing is no fun. It's only fun to have written.
—Dorothy Parker

There are many ways to mine your preferences. An immediate source of material, especially if you can't pinpoint your own interests yet, is your professors' current research or passions. Most professors conduct research or are vitally engaged in the area they specialize in. Ask them if you can help with their projects. Although this may sound intimidating, remember, professors can always use help; rarely do they have an adequate staff of researchers or assistants. By getting involved in a part of a large project, you can find out what roles attract you. Are you interested in:

- Research?
- Analysis?
- Interviewing?
- Writing?
- Organizing?

You'll also find out which topics capture your interest—and just as importantly, which don't.

No matter what you do, it's up to you to take the initiative. That means you have to start a discussion instead of waiting to be invited. All you have to do is drop in to your professors' offices during scheduled hours and ask what they're working on. Ask them if and where you can help. Perhaps you can expand upon an idea in one of your professor's papers. Sometimes, something else happens; your visit provokes a topic, which you and your professor will spin off, that neither of you would have thought of before. The very act of discussing your interests and you work also begins a mentor-protégé relationship with professors in powerful ways.

The Zero-to-One Rule

Remember the zero-to-one rule: It's a lot easier to get from one to two than it is to break the zero-to-one barrier. Getting started is always the hardest and most critical part.

The idea of building onto or jumping off from a professor's work is especially viable for graduate students who are searching for topics for their own theses and dissertations. There is, however, nothing stopping undergraduates from engaging in research as well. In fact, this type of collaboration can be a great spur to any undergraduate who intends to continue in the field. Each of the professors to whom I've spoken agrees with this point. And each has been instrumental in guiding interested undergraduates by helping them plan and prepare for graduate programs. Your willingness to take that first step is the key to making opportunities that would not otherwise exist for you—opportunities that can shape your future.

Career Qs

Q. I am an M.B.A. student with a full-time job. How can I ensure that this degree will provide advancement for me?

A. It will, but only if you make it pay off. But you can't just wait until your graduate program is over. Instead, use your program to launch you into the next kind of work you'd really like to be doing. If you want to stay at your company, then ask your bosses and theirs what they need to be researched. Or talk to them about which problems you'd like to tackle. You could also invite them to serve as guest speakers in your classes and continue your discussions at work. If you could involve your company in your program, using real issues as case studies, you would be launching yourself right in your own company—a true win-win situation.

However, if you want to use your M.B.A. degree to catapult you to another company or field, then consider using business school as the way to connect yourself to other companies. Think of a project that will propel you in the subject or role you aim for, either through interviewing or surveying people in other organizations. By meeting people doing the kind of work you admire, you'll build a network that will be valuable to you. By researching a topic or area, you identify opportunities. You could also build your reputation by publishing your papers in your company paper or a professional journal. By the time you complete your M.B.A., you'll have had experience in investigating and testing out real opportunities. When you graduate, you won't be just starting out.

Another challenging way to use your curriculum is to start developing your own specialization, something that compels you to further exploration, something perhaps that you intend to build your career around. Make that topic the "theme" of your major, even of all your course work. You can delve into different facets of your "theme" in every course requiring a paper. This is the double agenda at work: You can gain expertise in an area that is compelling to you while you're getting academic credit!

I learned the hard way in college, fulfilling the assignments I was given as well as I could and choosing electives that I loved—comparative religion, sculpture, geology—choosing an appropriate enough major, English, without thinking to build a career around them. Only later, when I went to graduate school, did I realize that I could have used the curriculum to develop my own talents and then to forge a career around them. By the time I was in a Ph.D. program, I became focused. Then each course's assignments became a means for me to explore the subject that had become my own calling—identifying other people's careering skills, from the history of how-to literature to the identification of skills for success through listening to the stories of those people who were fulfilled and those who yearned to be.

You might not be so definite about what you're after. Suppose you are an art education major wondering if you wouldn't be better off working in a business organization rather than teaching. Here are some ideas to help you clarify your choices and recognize that we can use the same talents and skills in a variety of careers. For instance, you might look into designing training aids, computer graphics, or developing management training programs. To find out what these careers are like, you can use assigned papers from your major or other classes to:

- Research the history and success rates of training aids or programs
- Compare product differences and similarities within one field (education) or among others (banking, museums, computers)
- Volunteer to work, paid or not, on an actual design project
- Interview local artists to find out how they exhibit and sell their work

Finally, take electives in related fields—art design, computer graphics, communication theory, or management courses in training or in the arts.

If you do investigate the possibilities latent in every kind of assignment, your course work and related activities will become personally challenging and engaging. They will catapult you into a field that is likely to be a good fit for you. Pursuing this kind of double agenda will permit you to develop aspects of your major or specialty before you graduate, or help you choose a program that's really right for you. There's wisdom in building onto your natural abilities rather than forcing yourself to fit what others think is the right course of action.

Phil's Story: The Psych Student Who Wasn't Psyched

This story shows the high cost of completing assignments for the sole purpose of getting the grade.

> Tired of graduate school and eager to get out to work, Phil, a psychology student, still had to face writing a dissertation. Instead of picking a subject that interested him or even related to the work he wanted to do, Phil merely chose a topic he thought would easily satisfy his professor. Then he undertook the usual laborious task of programming data—data, in this case, that he didn't care about in the first place but still had to spend endless, tedious hours analyzing.
>
> The result was predictable. He wrote a slipshod first draft that was turned down by his professor. He procrastinated doing the final draft because he was so bored. Phil is now a good candidate for that all-too-common degree, the A.B.D.—All-But-Dissertation. This nondegree typically goes to "good students" who haven't learned the self-reliance that underlies knowing how to choose topics that will work for them. Our psychology grad student will need a lot of motivation to jump-start his stalled career. If he doesn't, he'll brand himself a failure, living with downsized expectations the rest of his life.

Think of the waste of time, money, and hope. College is a time for personal direction finding, an education of the mind and heart. The lesson: Find something that beckons to you, compels you, and pursue it. And do it! If you can't identify something like that immediately, start searching. Talk to your professors and counselors about following a lead, branching off on a sideline. Professors and counselors can act as signposts, pointing out paths that you can investigate so that you can match your interests better. But you have to start with something at hand. Often making yourself go through the process of pursuit awakens buried interests or creates new ones.

Any paper you write for a professor requires time and effort, so why not put in a little extra effort and make it count doubly? Write your paper for two goals: for your professor, of course, but also for publication in a professional magazine, journal, or newspaper. Career counselor Sandi Silverman showed her senior history paper on jazz to her musician father who was so impressed with it that he submitted it to the *West Coast Rag;* they, in turn, published her paper in a seven-part series and offered her a job as well.

No matter whether you are in undergraduate or graduate school, and have to write a thesis or dissertation, you may have to write a major paper. To build toward it, you can start by writing about aspects of your thesis, or tackling segments of it, in classes along the way. Once you've identified you topic you've found your calling. Sometimes your research efforts can be transformed into a popular or commercial success, for example, Deborah Tannen's *You Just Don't Understand,* Beverly Kaye's *Up Is Not the Only Way,* or my *Skills for Success.*

Fred's Story: Double Major, Double Agenda

Class assignments themselves can be springboards to finding interests that can, in turn, lead to exciting careers.

> Fred is already a good writer, double majoring in history and business, but he doesn't have a clue what he'll do after graduation. By turning an assignment from any class into his own experiment, he could tap what interests him and generate ideas that can be refined into a career later on. For example, he could offer to write a history of a business's growth and learn business writing by doing. Then if the paper is really good, the company might want to publish it in its company newsletter, or help to get it published elsewhere. Fred's chances of being hired for the public relations or communications department of that company or a newspaper or business service immediately increases because he's proved his success.

This one paper, which earns Fred academic credit anyway, could also be a real launching pad to a new career in itself. It could catapult Fred into a career writing company histories or as a writer producing annual corporate reports. Or it can lead to other related fields. But Fred will never know unless he is willing to extend himself for an assignment. That means being serious about finding a topic that is personally engaging and actively researching it. It's part of what makes college so worthwhile.

Career Qs

Q. I have just finished writing my résumé and need to do a cover letter. What should I say on it that isn't on my résumé? Any help would be appreciated.

A. The cover letter is your chance to expand on and explain your major accomplishments that you haven't cited in your résumé. For example, you can always write a few sentence about how well you did in a few of your courses which you feel will prepare you for the job; for example, computer, finance, health, or sociology courses.

I hope you have been involved in cocurricular activities. If so, you could describe how you've demonstrated initiative, teamwork, leadership, and/or acquired experience with technology or budgets or negotiation. If you've held part- or full-time jobs, turn them into assets by explaining what you did and what you learned. This is a chance to expand beyond the truncated versions of your achievements on your résumés.

A cover letter also gives you the opportunity to call the prospective employer. Write a last paragraph saying something like, "Thank you for your consideration. I am excited about the opportunity to meet you and learn more about your needs. I will call you in a few days to follow up and set a convenient time for an interview."

Caution: Have someone credible (like your career counselor, professor, or employer) proof your letter and résumé before you mail it. Sloppy mistakes are not tolerated and will eliminate you immediately. And make yourself call in three days to follow up. It's always up to you to make it happen.

Papers that Launched People

A political science undergraduate in California studying the Middle East situation came up with an unusual solution for one aspect of its political strife. She sent her theory to the *Christian Science Monitor's* Op Ed page (the page opposite the editorials saved for opinions from individuals in the community). The paper printed it. Then, even more rewarding, a professor at a prestigious eastern university read it and was so impressed with her fresh ideas that he offered her a fellowship to study with him in a special master's program. She, of course, accepted enthusiastically. By having the courage to write and then to chance submitting her paper in the first place, she set off a chain of events that could not have happened if she had been merely content to sit back and settle for just an A.

The Teach for America program, which has put thousands of recent college graduates to work in poor schools throughout the country, sprang from Wendy Kopp's '89 senior thesis at Princeton. Wendy Kopp modeled her thesis's program on the Peace Corps's two-year service. Teach for America has since won presidential approval to join Americorps, President Clinton's national service initiative. Wendy's goal went way beyond fulfilling an assignment; she wanted to solve a nationwide need for teachers while creating leaders. In the process, she created an impressive and meaningful career.

Going Beyond the First Draft

While I can't offer any tips on how to write well, I can advise you to take courses in creative writing or journalism. I can only emphasize how difficult the process of writing is. To make matters worse, we have too little experience in the craft of writing. Most of us in college write our papers in one draft. Believing that is all there is to it, we turn in the paper, and wait to receive a grade. Yet real writers agree that writing is really rewriting. Students suffer from not learning how to write which leads to not learning how to think.

Therefore, let me offer one important although painful strategy: Make yourself discuss your paper with your professor. Go over the structure and details together. Learn how to rethink your ideas and rewrite them, *even though a second draft wasn't assigned or given credit*. In the process, you will not only become closer to your professor, you will learn how to develop and shape ideas. Francis Bacon advised in his famous essay: More than thinking or speaking, only writing makes you exact. There is another benefit, less obvious but just as important, that will stand you in good stead throughout your working life: You will learn to push yourself, putting aside your immediate ego needs for something that will become far more valuable to you. One reason many companies don't want to hire new graduates is that they come to work with the same attitude that they had in school—a "once is enough" syndrome. In every aspect of life—college, business, and in professional life, doing and redoing are what it takes to do a job well.

GO FORWARD WITH PROJECTS

Every course has its requirements—usually papers and exams, and sometimes projects. Occasionally you are able to substitute a special project for the more usual exam or paper. If so, do it because projects offer unique possibilities for you to explore interests first hand and develop connections to the outside world.

For example, if you are enrolled in business or management school, you can also learn to design surveys to cover such subjects as the philosophy of work, emerging employment, trends, comparative studies in productivity, the impact of new technologies and resulting new products, or the training of new workers. Through interviewing managers or employees the managers select to help you with your project and then sharing your results you'll reap several benefits. Besides learning from the experiences, your engagement also shows how you work and think. You can also invite several of the most impressive or inventive people to school on a panel where they can relate their experiences and ideas for your class. After you complete your project, and discover your interest in this aspect of information gathering or marketing, you can follow up by contacting the marketing, advertising, or human resources departments and get an edge on future employment.

Robert Haft's project for his Harvard M.B.A. program was to develop a business plan. Combining his personal knowledge of his family's discount pharmacy business with his keen interest in books, he created a plan for the first discount bookstore chain. Not only did that project satisfy his program requirements, but it generated his own successful business, Crown Books, a company that has revolutionized the bookselling industry.

Another Use for Your Student I.D.

You have a very real but invisible advantage as a student: People will answer your questions as soon as you identify yourself as one who is studying something related to their business. Your tag as "student" allows people to answer your questions and provide information that they'd never reveal to other inquirers who aren't students. Most successful people feel an obligation to assist you in college. Use this opening as an advantage to further your curiosity about procedures and markets, inventions and research that lead to opportunities.

And speaking of opportunities, know that they don't come labeled. They are disguised as obstacles or hard work and are clearly identified only in hindsight. Opportunities require a combination of risks and mental muscle.

Career Qs

Q. What exactly is the "hidden" job market?

A. Hidden is jobspeak for not advertised. This usage predates widespread access to electronic listings, like JOBTRAK. In low-tech days of yore, job searchers had to scour newspaper classified sections. But they discovered that only a small percentage of available jobs were advertised in this way. Finding great jobs, especially beyond entry level, required using face-to-face persuasion and working interpersonal relationships.

Looking for "hidden" or unadvertised jobs is still a great strategy. It still takes the push and pull of gutsy effort of asking a prospective employer for a chance—whether or not a job is open or even exists. It means meeting prospective employers through researching a paper or project, through interviewing or shadowing professionals to learn more about their business, or through real experience in an internship or part-time job. And it often requires tapping your friends and your family's friends for job leads and telling them about your skills and ambitions.

This approach is not so neat or easy as answering job listings, but it works more often and better.

WHAT YOUR CHOICE OF ELECTIVES CAN TEACH YOU

Just as there are behavioral skills to develop, so there are interests or purposes to pursue. You can't know what your interests all at once. You have to discover or confirm your interests through the choices you make and the actions you take to claim your mission in life. Keep this in mind when you're choosing electives. If you're an English major whose hobby is cooking, consider taking home economics courses to augment the possibilities of being a food or cookbook editor/writer, or a food stylist for commercials. If you're a science major, you may want to understand organizational theory as well as the theories of physics; you can, therefore, take business courses as electives. If you're an urban planning major, know that much in your field depends on persuasive negotiation and presentations before groups. Take every speech and debate course you can to enhance your skills.

Learn to pay attention to developing your interests—whether they're small inklings or full-fledged passions. Allow yourself the pleasure and luxury of pursuing that which calls or beckons you. Consider electives not as easy ways out, but as ideal ways to embroider your course of study with interests that make you more well-rounded and happy; more connected to yourself. To ignore your own interests is to lose yourself while you pretend to be someone else, someone who will only disappoint you.

EXAMS AND THE ART OF SELF-PRESENTATION

Now for that single task producing high anxiety—exams. Tests appear as regularly as clockwork; yet somehow taking them doesn't get any easier. Fear of being tested is profound. We are desperately afraid of failing to look good and appear smart. We fear falling short of an authority's expectations. This desperation pervades us and stops us from realizing what we do know and how we do think. Ironically, tests are the ideal forum for presenting what you have learned. From that point of view alone, they are valuable.

But there is another aspect of taking exams which is more subtle but equally as important as part of establishing your own double agenda. Learning how to present yourself on paper as well as in person is this critical aspect. Obviously I am not talking about objective tests—true-false or multiple-choice. For them, there is only one piece of advice I can offer—find out as much about the test in advance as you can. Talk to someone who has previously taken a test given by the specific instructor. Ask for samples of the test so that you can get the format. Search for patterns in answering. This information is easily accessible for required standardized exams such as the GRE, LSAT, or GMAT from the test makers' regularly released sample test questions. And of course, there is help from Kaplan in books, on computers, and through courses to help you prepare for such standardized tests.

But subjective tests, or essays, are quite a different matter. It is here that you have a chance to demonstrate your critical-thinking ability to your professors. The trick is not to answer like a robot, spewing out meaningless lists of data, but instead to offer a conceptual framework that shows that you are knowledgeable and curious.

Presenting facts within a significant framework requires definite skill. Some students who regularly get A's on their papers introduce their answers with a contemporary or classical theorist's quote or literary reference containing the essence of their response. By doing so, they demonstrate their ability to synthesize the material while providing a graceful opening. It is clear that they have taken the time before the test to do some research and include the views of theorists to show a grasp of both past and contemporary thinking. If they have strong preferences for one school of thought over another, they explain their reasons. In short, they demonstrate in writing to their professors that they not only have a knowledge of their material but also that they understand its significance.

Survey Responses: Major Decision

In our "Undergrad-itudes" survey, we asked the question, "How did you decide on your major?" Here's how the respondents answered.

Always interested	222
Inspired by professor	69
Advised by family	33
Guessed	18
Haven't decided yet	9
Chose something to get me accepted	8
Went with others	6

Oral Exams: Worse than Root Canal?

For most people, public speaking brings up the most terrible of fears. It's as if revealing what we think in front of others— being visible—exposes us to mortal danger. Whether the feeling is real or imagined, there are some ways to take action so that we can appear to be as smart and prepared as we are.

Courses in public speaking and debate help prepare students to develop skills in thinking clearly and in leadership. Make yourself sign up for such courses, even though they seem formidable. Going through the typical trauma of speaking in front of a class is actually quite therapeutic; everyone is in the same boat and cheers each other on. Public speaking provides invaluable training now and later in your career. Successful people become spokespersons for their companies, their industries, and usually in their communities. They are rewarded for presenting themselves with strength and grace. Learning how to do that early in college is one of the traits that successful people share.

How to Prep for an Oral Exam

There are several tactics that you can teach yourself, however. First, rehearse by listing possible questions that your professor or professors might pose. Then prepare *comprehensive* answers. You cannot answer in monosyllabic yeses or noes anymore than you can simply answer "I don't know." If you don't know an answer, begin your response by admitting that, then immediately elaborate how you would go about finding out, and where it fits into what you do know.

Tests are less about getting the critical fact out than they are about determining whether you can handle an answer, in short, whether you are knowledgeable.

You can practice your oral answers, just as you would written answers. Format an oral answer as you would an essay—have a beginning, middle, and end. You certainly can and should refer to the work of others, including that of the professor or professors you are addressing.

If you are a graduate student preparing for your orals, then you must also take responsibility for the exam session. What you are being judged on is not only whether you can remember every single detail but also whether you can present your facts in a meaningful framework. Let me repeat an incident, which was often misunderstood, that I included in *Skills For Success*. It's quite appropriate here.

A director of training of a major psychoanalytic institute told me about two young men who had just taken their oral examinations in order to be admitted to the institute. That means that about ten to twelve years after college, medical school, internship, residency, their own psychoanalysis, and several years of special training in the institute, these two men-in-training would again be test-ed to see if they could be admitted at last to the prestigious analytic institute.

As I did, you might assume that they would both pass, since they had the same years of training. But only one did. How was it possible to fail after so much extraordinary education and practice? I wanted to know the questions asked of the two men, and both the passing and failing responses. What I found out helps us understand the all-powerful nature of self-presentation.

There was only one question. It was asked of both men independently: "What would you expect a one-year-old baby to do if its mother, upon bringing it to your office, had to leave the room for a few minutes?" The following is the *fail-ing* response: "I'd expect the baby to cry after being separated from the moth-er." The *passing* answer: "I'd expect the baby to cry after being separated from the mother. Separation anxiety is maybe the most complex issue of all our lives, especially obvious in infancy. There are, however, conflicting interpreta-tions. According to these . . . ."

So let's look at what happened. At first glance, it appears that the psychiatrists' answers are identical. The facts are there; both agree that the baby cries. But any serious interview or exam doesn't measure only one's ability to state a fact. Often the *facts* themselves are less important than the *interpretation* of them, especially in the art of psychiatry. The failing psychiatrist gave an answer and waited obediently. The passing one posited the same answer but then revealed what it meant through a series of interpretations. He provided a way to let the examiner know that he was prepared, having studied and read others' work extensively. He spoke as a colleague and as a likely credit to the institute. He knew intuitively that the test was a vehicle for such self-presentation.

What the examiner wanted to ask, but legally could not, was, "Are you enough like us to warrant our letting you join our institute?" The first psychiatrist was not; he proved himself still a student, waiting for the next question which never came. But the second candidate was. In addition to knowing the facts, he also knew how to substantiate his answer with examples from psychiatric theory and practice. The director knew the difference between the answers and consequent-ly between the trainees; he chose his colleague to join him, not his student.

All subjective tests, whether written or oral, are vehicles for self-presentation. The questions are there to provoke a dialogue—a vehicle giving you an oppor-tunity to reveal who you are and what you know.

There are behaviors we can and must learn. We want not only to be successful students but successful protégés and, thereafter, successful professionals. We cannot wait until the last minute to learn the appropriate behavior. These behaviors encompass skills that must be developed, just as in sports. If you want to be an expert skier, would you put on a pair of skis and ski for the first time in front of a judge? That is, of course, preposterous. Yet that is exactly what we demand of ourselves in pressured tests, written or oral. We need practice and coaching. And it is up to us to get it.

STRATEGIES FOR CREATING A DOUBLE AGENDA

Here are some tips on using academic assignments strategically.

1. If it's required, do it. But do it with heart.

2. If the assignment's harder than ones you're used to, go see your professor. Even though it's embarrassing to ask for help, you'll pull through—a far better alternative to failing. Something else happens: Your professor is likely to become more invested in your efforts to succeed and offer more help and understanding.

3. If you can't complete the assignment or take the test because of some emergency, talk to your professors. If you leave a message, but your professors don't call you back, call again and again; go to their offices again and again. How often? Until you see them and make up your work. Don't ignore this seemingly unpleasant task of explanation and negotiation with you professors or it will cost more than you can imagine.

4. Worst-case scenario? You flunk a test or an assignment. What then? Ask how you can make it up, take it over, complete another one. Don't ignore it! Don't give up. Then the failure will turn into one of those events that you realize only later (true, a lot later) helped you to grow.

5. Sometimes your past record isn't a reflector of your present ability. You might have goofed off in high school or, more likely, in your freshman year, and now you've turned into a great student. Each semester you can make a fresh start! Do it now, magnificently.

6. Ambition is a great stressor; use its adrenaline!

Chapter Four
Turning Your Professors into Mentors

Life is not complete until you acquire a master.
—Shri Satyapal Ji

Relationships are tricky things. No getting around that. The interpersonal dynamics—of hope and betrayal—between friends and lovers have been the subject of books, songs, and movies. But the relationship between student and professor is a unique one complicated by its complete inequality in power.

LEAVING HOME

The family model is the most familiar. What's supposed to happen is for parents to provide their children with emotional and financial support as preparation for eventual independence. But, in fact, parents worry that children are self-indulgent, rebellious, complaining, boring, demanding, nonsupportive, and blaming. While parents hope that their children become independent and successful, they simultaneously want to keep them obedient, grateful, and loving.

On the flip side, as sons and daughters, we painfully learn to separate ourselves from blind obedience and dependency. We want independence and struggle to find ourselves yet at the same time we see-saw, still relating to our parents as children.

But how do we relate to our professors? We have no real guidelines. If you look around your class or seminar, I'd bet you'd see a range of behaviors, from quite passive to rebellious, exhibited by students who have not yet separated their teachers from their parents.

For a better model for interaction, consider the relationship of *apprentice* to *master,* closer to what a productive student-professor relationship can be. In the model dating back to preindustrial times young apprentices became indentured servants to master artists or craftsmen in order to learn their trades. Performing menial tasks at first, apprentices learned to develop their skills to a master level at which time they were able either to take over or go out on their own. The same kind of system was applied in higher education, but we have lost sight of this historical fact. To benefit, put your professors in the role of master and play the part of apprentice—just leave out the indentured servant part. Then as you can identify what you'd like to learn, you can reap the great rewards in store.

BUILDING THE RELATIONSHIP

Other people can't make you see with their eyes.
At best, they can encourage you to use your own.
—Aldous Huxley

Once you find professors whom you respect, it is then up to you to initiate the relationship. The best way is to hang out in their offices during office hours and talk to them. Ask your professors for their own stories or experiences; for advice or support on a specific problem; to elaborate on anecdotes they told in class. Professors schedule times when you can meet them in their offices for just this purpose. Or you can catch them in their departmental offices. You can usually act on any of the following:

- Take as many courses as possible from the professors you're interested in.
- Read their published papers and books.
- Go to your professors' offices to discuss academic as well as other topics.
- Talk informally with your professors after class.

In short, demonstrate your interest. Your professors will not only get it but also appreciate it. They'll start coaching you. Don't think of cultivating your professors in this way as brownnosing. Rather, it's building your first network of value!

After having interviewed so many successful managers, artists, and professionals I've learned that they each had had several mentors who were critical to their business and personal development. These mentors were helpful in identifying their talents and encouraging their skill development. These mentors also helped them by pointing out careers which they might not have thought of on their own, and then they connected them to opportunities through researchers and prospective employers. In this very same way, you can turn professors into your mentors and learn how to build on what you have learned and apply it in appropriate directions. The alternative? To sit in class, taking notes, with a sign pasted on your forehead that says, "Ignore me. Pass on any opportunities to someone else."

Survey Responses: Who Talks to Teachers?

In our "Undergrad-itudes" survey, we asked the question, "Have you ever spoken with professors out of class?" Here's how the respondents answered.

Talked about academic subjects with interest and still do	120
Asked for help and was satisfied	100
Never	35
Asked for help but was disappointed	4

A highly acclaimed computer analyst told me that his career had actually been formed because of one charismatic and brilliant professor. As a student, he was clearly awed, coming to class early and staying late to discuss the problems he had been working on. During that year, the professor encouraged him to change his major from industrial engineering to economics, introduced him to a prominent professor in graduate school who offered him a fellowship for advanced study. He couldn't have done any of this on his own. Other students thought he was just *lucky* that he had been singled out because he was talented. It's easy to think that, but it's not altogether true. There are, after all, many good students. The reason that this student was "chosen" was due to the effort he had made to do the "choosing" himself.

In the same way, a well-known headhunter in the field of industrial design was boosted in her design studies and in her behavior skills by her mentor, the only woman on the faculty at her college. This professor, a role model for so many other female students, knew how difficult it would be for young women to be accepted in the business world. The professor's mentoring of the aspiring executive included socializing. She met with her student and gave help and advice over long lunches—complete with tips on etiquette—for more than a decade after the student graduated.

It's hard to admit that we each crave this unique relationship and even harder to think of why any professor would want to invest time in us. But the truth is such relationships are really mutually beneficial. If you believe that you are only imposing on a professor's valuable time, you'll make it harder for yourself. In fact, it works in just the opposite way. Know that you will be, in great part, helping both of you. You need mentors, and professors need protégés like you. Many live in a theoretical world of research: Their success depends so much on their reputation as significant thinkers and on their ability to attract funding. Grants and contracts secured by professors represent a major source of revenue for universities. Student tuition, surprisingly, contributes a much smaller percentage towards the operating costs of any university.

The professor's second world is political. It encompasses responsibilities on academic committees and within university associations as well as administrative duties within a department. These tasks are time-consuming and usually obligatory. Who then provides necessary positive feedback that professors need to carry on? In part, you do, as vitally interested, gifted, willing students.

Also keep in mind that professors love being able to shape students' lives. This is why they chose to teach in the first place. By recognizing that the student-professor relationship is reciprocal, you will be able to give more. And your professors will be able to give more in return.

Annette's Story: A Professor Intervenes

Sometimes professors can help even with seemingly insurmountable personal problems, as the following story shows.

> Annette was studying art history when a family problem arose that would have cost her an entire college education had it not been for the intervention of one of her professors. When Annette's father fell ill and lost his job, the family was unable to make its mortgage payments, let alone meet the daughter's tuition. Panicked, Annette was considering quitting to find a full-time job in order to support her family. Her favorite art profes-

sor rescued her. He convinced her to stay on by helping her get a fifty percent scholarship and a part-time job at night as a guard. The job allowed her some time to study—a perfect arrangement. The continuous moral support that her professor provided was also vital to Annette's college career, which turned out to be extraordinary, including honors, grants, and two articles co-authored with her mentor.

RETURNING STUDENTS

Some cautions: Finding a professor-mentor is often harder for older nontraditional students. Once a small percentage of the student body, older students are now the norm. But being the same age as one's professor can be initially uncomfortable for both sides. Returning students often make two basic errors—sometimes overplaying but more often underplaying their role. While they might feel they should be more collegial, returning students still have to seek advice and guidance. But they shouldn't make the mistake, in their terror of failing, of falling back into a completely subservient student role. And it is easy to slip and regress from their real age of thirty or forty to become anxious eighteen-year-olds, reverting to the emotional age they were when they were last in school. Easy to do, easy to understand, but still a costly mistake.

Career Qs

Q: I am an returning student in my 30s and want help in finding career direction, but I don't have a clue about where to go for this help.

A: You have several options. Go to your career center. Sign up for a career assessment workshop, and then make an appointment with a career counselor. To choose a career, you'll start a search for every avenue. You never know where that perfect idea for you will come from.

Much like divorced people starting to date again at forty, returning students suddenly find themselves with the same fears they had when they were eighteen. Just being aware of this awkward phenomenon happening to everyone, you'll understand your overwhelming anxiety. Being aware lets you take steps to calm down enough so that you can act appropriately. I know it's hard. Most returning students, not to mention traditional students, experience strange mood swings. Here's what happens if you deny the anxiety you feel. You are often tempted to dazzle your professors with your own prior successful experiences in order to prove your worth. Unintentionally, you are only creating a competitive situation.

Roberta's Story: Back to School

The following story shows some of the perils peculiar to older students returning to school.

> At thirty-eight, Roberta had come back to school to study psychology at the graduate level after some years' of administrative work at a mental health clinic. She claimed that her hardest adjustment to school lay in being offended by some of the simplistic, redundant ideas her professors presented to students who had never even seen a mental health environment. While her professor had theoretical research on his side, he had never run such a clinic. Imagine Roberta's holding forth in a debate or constantly trying to have the last word in class, as she wanted to do. Instead she had to learn to let go of her need to prove herself right. She had to find an appropriate balance so that she could bring her own experience to class yet still show her respect for her professors. To her surprise, she had to master a new diplomacy. Had she not, she would have broadcast the message: "I know more about this subject than you do. I am just taking this course because it's required. But I resent your not teaching me anything new."

How else could Roberta have used and even benefited from her past work experience? She might have invited feedback on how to handle situations in which the mental health clinic staff was stuck with a problem. Or she could have reflected about her unique experiences as an administrator serving psychologists and psychiatrists working with specific groups of people and revealed some of their successes and failures. Or, she might have suggested a pilot research program to train administrators to be counselors.

Career Qs

Q. I am a reentry student and need to spend my evenings studying. But my husband who is also a student doesn't understand my needs. I feel so guilty. Any suggestions?

A. This is a difficult but resolvable dilemma. You'll have to act as the change agent, the management motivator. Plan a weekly time-management meeting with your husband. Ask him to stipulate the daily times he will devote to work and study; you do the same. Remember to block out times for cooking, shopping, and studying. Then chart the time you can spend together.

Set aside at least thirty minutes together every evening. Divide the time in half so that you can take turns telling each other about your separate activities. Be careful not to waste time complaining, or let your time together dwindle away as the semester wears on and you get even busier. Be dedicated to your agreed schedules. Don't let either of you settle for worse behavior than you'd tolerate at work or school. Be sure to compliment each other saying out loud why you love each other. Remember, you deserve time to study without feeling guilty; seclude yourself by closing your door or going to the library. You'd do—or have already done—the same for him. Expect the same respect.

WHAT YOU CAN DO

Start taking the risk of forming relationships with one or more of your professors. In the beginning, it's likely to feel uncomfortable, even frightening, but that's true for all new and worthwhile pursuits. In actuality, the risk is so minimal compared to the potential rewards. Be fair to yourself; you are not stupid, or you wouldn't be in college in the first place. Wanting to learn more is the reason you're in school. Start by confronting your own fears. *One of the traits that separates those who are stuck from the achievers is that achievers try for more even when they are afraid, whereas the stuck people stop themselves with their fear.* Mark Twain said it well, "Courage is not the absence of fear, but the mastery of it."

Limits

A word of caution is necessary here. Too much of a good thing is not so good. Turning a professor into a god who has all the answers is not healthy or productive. It violates a basic ethical code and precludes any meaningful exchange of ideas. The same goes for turning your professor into a lover. Attaching yourself to professor-mentors you respect for their intelligence and knowledge is not the same as hero worship or infatuation. But it is possible that you will become entranced by a seemingly ideal professor. If this happens, know that it's an ordinary reaction, a phase to be lived through. Like the apprentice, as you develop your expertise, you will eventually stand next to your professor as an equal. These are natural phases of our growth, from which we shouldn't shy away.

Claude's Story: Learning the Dynamics

This story is a kind of best-case scenario, illustrating the rewards that can come from building a mentor relationship with a professor.

> Claude, a graduate student in sociology, became a research assistant to a top, grant-getting professor at a major state university. While assigned to what seemed like a relatively insignificant task in one area of data collections, Claude saw where he could contribute more than the job required. He could coordinate the schedules and chart the progress of the other data-collecting student researchers. By developing a specialized role for himself, Claude soon became indispensable. Furthermore, he enrolled in all of the professor's courses over the following several years so he could continue learning more about his professor's theories and continue working for him. Claude made it part of his day to stop by his professor's office casually to talk about assignments and research as well as daily life.
>
> For all his efforts, Claude got so much in return. His rewards lay not just in raises and a full scholarship, though they were tremendously helpful. But he was also given a section of his professor's project to work on. That included a grant to support himself, with a topic for his thesis, which in turn let him to an impressive doctoral program. More than getting a scholarship and research project, Claude had the rich opportunity to watch a successful professor at work in academia. Claude observed

his professor in the process of writing and getting grants, implementing major research, and involved in reciprocal relationships with other professionals in that university and across the country. In addition, he was also privy to the way the professor acted politically in his voluntary-but-necessary major committees of tenure and development. Claude witnessed his professor's successful style of decision making. Then when Claude himself was ready to apply for a doctoral program, his mentor personally referred him to a team of world-famous professors who had even more connections to offer. The sponsorship of Claude's first professor was the catapult to Claude's progress in his field. No student with only straight A's could have gained so much.

Do you think that what Claude did to get his initial job was worth the risk? "What risk?" you might ask. Claude took the chance of being called a brownnoser by some cynics in his class. Not only did Claude survive any name calling, but he succeeded far beyond any of his disdaining peers. They self-righteously refused to "use" their professors, and their refusal cost them their professional lives. At the end of the term, some of the nonconnected, "good students" did have grades to be proud of. But here's what they *didn't* have: references, exposure to new people who could open doors, or new insights beyond their rigorously studied discipline. The cynics were badly hurt by their beliefs that school is only for passing tests and getting grades. Ultimately, it is they who misuse the system when they fail to recognize their part in this human enterprise of higher education.

Career Qs

Q. I don't know if my major is the right one for me. How do I make sure?

A. Here are five tips to start your search for your calling:

1. *Ask your professors whether they think your major is right for you. But understand that you have to get them to know you well before they can they give relevant advice.*

2. Write an assigned paper either on a topic you'd like to explore in your major, or in another discipline that appeals more to you. For example, for a political science paper, report on the local office of a national political campaign, Democrat or Republican, or on the fundraising campaign of a city charity or public network. You'll get involved and learn about a **bigger** (better or worse) career than you'd imagined.

3. Find an internship or part-time job to get your feet wet in a field you're potentially interested in. While you're there, collect people's experiences and advice.

4. Join a club around your major and become active. For example, use the Journalism Club's program committee to question reporters or professionals about their careers or the Management Club's employers list for informational interviews.

5. Take one of the vocational tests offered in the career center. Review the results with your assigned counselor. Use this information as a guide to lead you to a career or away from one. Discuss choosing or changing your major.

Why do these things? To develop the megaskill of taking risks to link yourself to real activities done by real people working in their fields. Only then can you begin to find out what compels you. You cannot choose in a vacuum. And, the more active you are, the more you'll learn about yourself.

SIGNIFICANT OTHERS

Professors are not the only people on campus whose friendship you'll want. Speakers who visit a campus can be approached by introducing yourself after their lecture and then following up later with a letter which can open with "We met at . . . ." Your advisors, department heads and their staff are also knowledgeable and helpful. University administrative assistants are responsible for student activities, records, and grants, can be tremendously helpful to you in ways that your professors, whose expertise is usually confined to their areas of study, cannot.

For example, if you need encouragement or advice, the student activities staff provide miracles every day. If you are requesting special permission to take a course not usually open to you, or you need to petition to receive credit for a past course, your best bets lie with administrators who usually know the rules of the game, however much it changes, and can show you the best way to present your case or yourself. If you need financial aid, fellowships, grants, or work-study, go to the financial aid staff.

Think of these administrators, counselors, and professionals as friends who can be there to help you. Don't wait until you're in the middle of a crisis to pay them a visit. They will be better equipped to provide assistance when you really need it if they already know who you are. That's true for everyone. But whenever you do need help, see these people. They can change the course of your life.

Family: The Original Network

Most of us have wished for different families, or at least ones that were more successful and well connected, more encouraging and supportive—financially, intellectually, and socially. And sometimes we strike out—but it's so hard for us to accept advice that we refuse the invitations to talk to our family or their networks for information about educational opportunities or career leads. We flat out turn them down believing that we'll do better—or at least differently—on our own. Of course, we just might, but we give up a lot by overlooking these sources.

Your family experience is a whole lot different from those well-worn T.V. sitcoms. There's a good chance your parents are divorced, or have experienced being downsized, or as anxious about their own future as they are about yours. Their questions about the immediate, pragmatic use of your major and their demands that your major lead directly to a secure career are sometimes out of kilter to your own searches. If it helps any, keep in mind that friction between parents' expectations and their offsprings' choices is legendary. It's been going on for thousands of years. We are familiar with the biographies of artists pursuing their path against their parent's objections. For example, composer Robert Schumann yearned to pursue his art but found himself at war with his parents, who wanted him to be a lawyer—a stable, respectable profession. Handling parental conflicts requires the most delicate negotiation you'll ever be called upon to perform. Sometimes you can make deals, and sometimes not. And when you can't decide at all, you can take a battery of psychological, ability, and vocational tests to demonstrate your own strengths and confirm your choice to yourself and to your family. Sometimes you fulfill both agendas and take a double major. Opposing your parents can be expensive if it comes down to paying for your education yourself, but it may be worth the investment. Don't try this alone; go talk to a psychologist or career counselor.

Many of you are experiencing college as the first in your families to attend. As first-generation students, you might find that your parents often can't give relevant real-world advice and are often off the mark about what college should do and provide. When that happens, you have to make yourself find the most appropriate advice and follow it; that often means educating your parents, the farthest thing from your own agenda. Sometimes they hold to their own vision. Their stubbornness, after all, has strength to it; it led them to educating you. The phrase *rendering unto Caesar Caesar's due* translates well for just this kind of dilemma. In this context it means learning the high skill of satisfying authority's demands while at the same time satisfying your own needs. It's not easy, but it's possible.

STRATEGIES FOR CULTIVATING MENTORS

Get to know your professors. Don't expect them to discover your talents and point you in the right direction. They won't. That is, they can't, not until you reveal yourself to them through open-ended discussions during office hours or after class. Ask to be a research associate, attend professional meetings, help with any tasks in return for the chance to hang around with significant people in your field. Working for free is better than not working at all. After all, it connects you to ideas and people who can, in turn, help and inspire you.

Chapter Five
The "Hidden Curriculum" of Clubs and Activities

*Action may not always bring happiness; but there is
no happiness without action.*
—Benjamin Disraeli

We need to develop a wardrobe of personalities and personal action. One of the best ways, if not the best way, for students to begin to find and practice these behaviors is through engaging in extracurricular activities. In that context, we can discover when we can be forceful and when not to be, when to take the lead and when to be supportive, how to handle conflict within a group, including when to ignore it. It's critical to develop these skills as the basis of our adult personal style. In fact, they are life skills, skills which we can start developing in college.

Clubs and activities are typically called *extra-* or *co-* curricular activities. Don't be fooled by the *extra,* which suggests that these are not part of the *real* curriculum. Clubs and activities offer a kind of "invisible" or "hidden" curriculum that complements what you learn in the classroom. Clubs and activities teach you how to talk to and work with people—something that can't be learned while listening to a lecture. And yet, in the real world, good communication skills are at least as important as the ability to do the job.

Each extracurricular event has many aspects that you can get involved in—far more than just the subject matter of the activity. For example, radio and baseball offer programs you have to plan, budgets to sort out, advertising and publicizing to do, and people to manage in addition to the chance to be a deejay or catcher. You can learn so much from getting involved in any of these aspects. What you gain in experience can come only by the actual doing. And there's no shortcut for it. College is the perfect place to start to practice these skills. Because it is so unlikely that you will be fired from a club or activity, you can feel free to experiment so much more than you would dare to on a first job with so many others who share your goals. And experimentation, risk taking, will be valued so much more in your later work.

Here is some of the leadership skills that you'll learn from the "hidden curriculum" of clubs and activities.

- You can learn how to motivate a group when its esprit lags and how to influence a group of people to do more.

- You can learn "win-win" negotiating skills; consensus and compromise making, and grow beyond always needing to be right, even at the expense of proving others wrong.

- You'll practice the critical arts of collaboration and teamwork.

- You'll gain experience in the difficult task of redirecting a project when it turns awry.

- And last but not least, you'll get to sample some career choices in a natural way.

At a recent focus group of employers I attended, every single one stressed the importance of extracurricular activities for students who are involved in clubs to demonstrate that they are responsible, motivated, and willing to go beyond what's expected. A leading biotech company recently had a slide presentation of what qualities the company was searching for in recruiting a thousand students: Team-building and communication skills were at the top of the list.

My interviews with successful people prove repeatedly that no one becomes successful overnight. No matter whether they were businesspeople, artists, or scientists, their ability to make the right decisions—often forging critical turning points in their lives—was always based on earlier, preparatory steps they had taken. For many, actions they had taken in high school and college had built their courage to take risks and to persevere through difficult times. Successful people whom I've observed have built up their expertise through the years, and continue to cultivate their skills and knowledge. They are always preparing for the next step, whether consciously or not, even if they haven't known what that next step will be. The achievers I interviewed have all tried out these strategies through their extracurricular activities.

What's in a list of activities? While it's true that some students will join clubs only to add to their résumé or yearbook, the majority of achievers I interviewed always did so much more than just join. They all made something happen no matter where they were. And making things happen—participating—is a great skill in itself. It's the foundation of building personal courage, personal mastery.

Learning how to create opportunities is a major life skill, one that can be developed. A cautionary word: The extraordinary effort engagement requires is worth it even if you have to defend your involvement to your friends or family for taking time away from your studies. No doubt you'll be swamped with obligations, but that can serve to make you better at managing your time and becoming more efficient at studying. Extracurricular activities and clubs have proved to be the touchstones upon which so many successful people have based their continuing experiences. Achievers specifically credit their college extracurricular activities for developing three different skills that stand them in great stead throughout their lives:

- Building personal courage
- Developing organization savvy or a sense of how to play "office politics"
- Establishing their first sense of real professionalism

These key factors are not yet typically taught in college, not even in M.B.A. programs or law school—though they certainly belong there. Academic learning needs to be and will be integrated with an awareness of how things work in the world. And it's happening, for example, through programs such as service learning which allow students to perform service work in the community as part of their academic course work.

DEVELOPING A WARDROBE OF BEHAVIORS

By the time we are in college, most of us already have developed a sense of style, of fashion. Each of us knows what to wear and when to wear it. We are able to choose clothes that are appropriate to the weather, or situation—interview suits, formal attire, beachwear. You can bet that opportunities in later life will keep changing our sense of style. So what we wear for a first job will definitely be different from what we wear a few years down the line in a higher-level position. Fashion is a symbol. But ultimately the phrase *apparel often proclaims the man* was wrong advice, as specious as the rest that the double-dealing Polonius gave to Hamlet.

Costly the habit as thy purse can buy, but not express'd in
fancy; rich, nor gaudy . . . For the apparel proclaims the man."
—Shakespeare, Hamlet

Putting on a three-piece suit may get you in the interview door, but it does not guarantee that you'll get (or stay) hired for the job you want, or get into graduate school.

What counts more than your clothing is your self-presentation, your behavior. Your account of who you are, what you've learned, and what you'll contribute. But there is too little training in developing a "wardrobe of personal behaviors." Mostly you develop only one way of interacting, and as a result, get stuck acting that one way for a lifetime. If you're obliging and unthreatening, you are always considered sweet and supportive. If you are angry or difficult, arrogant or abrasive, you play out that personality like a broken record.

Psychologists have always theorized about personality, debating whether it's inherited or learned from people around us, our family and friends. How does one develop a particular style? Is it calculated or does it just happen? Or do we pick it up from T.V. and other media? Or is it a combination of all these factors? No matter how we develop our personality, we can always modify aspects of it, yet we usually don't. We are more willing to change our hairstyle than we are our behavior. Most of us act as if personality were given, fixed, and not to be experimented with.

But observe how different we are when we are selling a car from when we are buying one, or when we are talking to our professors or to our parents, or to those students who are more knowledgeable than others. Does this mean that we are chameleons, or jellyfish lacking the rigid steel rod of character? On the contrary, it indicates that we naturally adapt and develop appropriate roles that enable us to choose what roles to enact, taking appropriate cues from the situation at hand. You might argue that this sounds too manipulative. But isn't it wiser to take charge of a situation than to be locked into only one way of acting or, worse, reacting? Performing our typical reactions like a robot removes the joy of spontaneous reaction, not only for you, but also for the people around you. And that robs you, leaves you totally predictable, which in turn ultimately makes you powerless—bored and boring.

Jim's Story: Engineering a Change

Let's look at the change in a top engineering student who had wanted to be an engineer ever since childhood.

> Jim's father had shared and encouraged his son's dream of a career in engineering as a means of escape from a limited, rural background. Had he kept his early dream intact, blinded to any other possibility, he would be an engineer today. That isn't a bad choice. But good choices have more to do with combining abilities with personal interest. Actively involved in student politics, Jim became a campus leader when college life was rolling along smoothly.
>
> His position, however, required him to resolve and mediate conflicts between officers, deal with a few unpopular issues, apprise his sponsors and professors of the student body government decisions, and invite provocative guests to campus meetings. From the simple act of becoming student body officer, Jim discovered new potential in himself. He became a confident leader with a pronounced talent for management. He tried out a new role and succeeded in it.
>
> There are always trade-offs in life. Jim paid the price. He sacrificed straight-A grades and nearly lost his chance for the one engineering position he really wanted. The engineering company hired him anyway because they were more impressed with his political experience than his GPA. They placed him in a management program. Today he heads a major program at one of the nation's leading organizations. Looking back, he recognizes that having been student body president changed his entire life.

Dramatic Results for Drama Club Members

Most of the successful lawyers I have interviewed attributed their skills at persuading juries and judges, as well as presenting themselves forcefully to clients and other lawyers, to their early active participation in drama club. Acting, they claimed, helped them to break out of their shells. That lawyers are interested in acting should not be so surprising. After all, you could say the courtroom itself creates dramatic situations. What experience tells us is verified by one of the major occupational classification systems; the Holland occupational code for lawyers is the same as it is for actors.

Clearly, drama clubs are good training grounds for both future lawyers and actors. But think of the possibilities for most anyone else—business, science, and art majors, too. Besides learning some of the great works of world literature, which are not usually taught in regular courses, drama clubs offer a good first step in career advancement—learning to overcome the fear of being in front of an audience.

Survey Responses: Clubs and Activities

In our "Undergrad-itudes" survey, we asked the question, "Which extracurricular activities have you chosen?" Here's how the respondents answered.

Response	Number of People
Sports	102
Greek	60
Philanthropy	56
Government	50
Business	48
Religious	48
Arts/Literature	42
Political	40
Performing Arts	40
Media	35

John and Carol's Stories: Showing Up Versus Participating

What you get out of an activity depends on what you put into it, as these next stories show.

John joined the Future Teachers of America Club even though he was not overly excited about the prospects of becoming a member of what he regarded as a limited profession. He joined with half a heart and, I might add, with only half a mind. Mentally absent during the meetings he attended, he went through the motions of being a member. He paid his dues and attended the meetings, but sat in them like the proverbial bump on a log, volunteering nothing, chairing nothing, contributing nothing, asking nothing. After graduation, he was unable to find a teaching job that suited him. It wasn't that the field of education was a bad choice. It's that John didn't take advantage of his chances.

Carol, the president of that same club, had an entirely different result. She applied for teaching positions in the public school system and at a community college system. Because she had already established a reputation prior to graduation, she was accepted by both school systems. How did she do this? Over her last few years at school, she had invited guests, both teachers and department chairs, to speak to the club. She stayed in contact with these people. She researched alternative curriculums for colleges and wrote papers about them. She familiarized herself with the different jobs of president, counselor, and instructor at liberal arts colleges and community colleges. She created opportunities for club members through a variety of internships. She sponsored a series of dinner meetings with faculty so that active students could learn more about the inside world of higher education. Finally, she asked the influential people she had come to know to write letters of recommendation for her; they responded positively. So it was much more than luck that landed Carol her first full-time college teaching position—though it seemed that way to people who didn't know her well.

Let's compare these two antithetical experiences. John came to the club expecting to be "done to"—informed, educated, placed, and launched—while Carol came to create something and help build a successful group. The Future

Teachers of America Club, like every organization, offered each member the same opportunities. One took advantage and benefited; the other did not.

If you want something to happen, you have got to make it happen. This sounds clichéd, but it is true. Life is indeed what you make it. Certainly we can all see this with our perfect twenty-twenty hindsight. Kierkegaard wrote that we understand life only in reverse, but we are forced to live it forward. We can, however, benefit from others' experiences, and we often do if we're smart.

Furthermore, we can each set up experiments for ourselves. We can begin with clubs and activities, internships, part-time jobs, courses, and seminars, seizing chances to shape and reshape ourselves according to what we want most. It all has to do with our intent to try, at the risk of making fools of ourselves, to create our own possibilities.

Career Qs

Q. How do I know which job objective to write on my résumé? If I'm applying for several jobs, do I need to write a different one for each?

A. You don't have to include your job objective on your résumé at all. At this point in your life, your résumé can be fairly standard: a one-pager including your education, work, internships, and volunteer and extracurricular activities with a separate sheet of references.

However, your cover letter is a different matter. It's your personal statement and must be individually written for each job you apply for. It's here that you state what you're applying for, why you're interested and qualified. It has to sound like your best self, not canned nor overly modest or boastful. Everyone who's written these and gotten the job knows how difficult the process is. So, don't do it alone or without a competent editor. Your career center will have samples of résumés and cover letters and can provide quick assistance. Take advantage of the resources there for you.

The Unemployed Ph.D. Club

Times have been hard—even Ph.D.'s often cannot find the teaching or research positions that their training prepared them for. Many have had to pursue other careers when they have been unemployed for months. To change that situation, a group of unemployed Ph.D.'s, graduates of a major institution, formed an association, the purpose of which was to make their plight public. They were sympathetically interviewed in the local newspapers and talk shows. They held monthly meetings and invited guest speakers to help them.

I was one such speaker. As I began to present alternatives to teaching, I noticed that the graduate students were recording my presentation for their newsletter. It seemed odd, but they were behaving like any association—trying to improve themselves, expand in size and scope, including producing a comprehensive monthly newsletter. But this was a group that should have expected to dissolve once the members could find jobs! Perhaps a more productive course would have been getting into the career development business. They could have invited each member who did find work to come back with a map of what he or she actually did, or sought help in starting up a short internship program to fuse academic theory with business practice. They could have linked up chemistry Ph.D's with oil companies; sent applied-art grads to advertising agencies; and matched historians with corporate libraries or newspapers.

Why didn't they do this? As high-minded academicians they held the business community in contempt. But with universities not hiring professors, they needed to reexamine their beliefs in order to achieve their goal of employment. Had they used their university time more creatively and productively, allowing time for varied activities, they might well have had a broader view of alternatives. Had they participated in extracurricular activities, their connections and experiences might have provided the employment opportunities they sought.

Direction Finder

You don't have to make only one choice. Know that you can and will be many things in this life. You may wear several hats at the same time, and then you may change direction altogether. But you must begin, and begin somewhere. You might start by becoming involved in several different efforts so that you can find out what appeals to you. Then you can decide to what extent you want to be involved. You will find that participating in athletics and music is quite different from the production of a radio show or newspaper or running for a student political office.

But you will find that your participation in athletics or the performing arts is not limited by your athletic ability or performing talents. You have to have what it takes to be part of a group that essentially creates harmony together, no matter whether it is a symphony orchestra, a jazz band, football team, or debating club. All of these activities offer the possibility of a great many different kinds of experiences. An All-American basketball star told me that his greatest learning experience came surprisingly during the time when he was benched. Despondent during that difficult year, he learned to cheer on his team members. Only after being there for them could he understand that a large part of his value and purpose came in supporting his team members not just playing well himself. On any athletic team, there are players who are known as the best performers, the most valuable, the most supportive or popular, the manager, the publicist—and each of them complements the team.

Understanding who we are and how we fit in is vital to our own development. But how do we learn these things? For example, if you are a member of the band but not the leader, you still have many chances to contribute. You may be the one who finds unusual music, the one who gets the campus newspaper to review the group, or the one who contacts professional musicians off campus to listen to and advise the group. Or, you might be the one who cooks chili and generates enthusiasm, support—the real esprit de corps.

The production of a campus newspaper or radio show offers a variety of jobs. If you are creative, you can be writer, performer, or both. If you are interested in public relations and advertising, you can assume the responsibility of selling the production to the potential audience and, in doing so, learn about the world of public relations or advertising. If you are interested in management, that chance exists, along with the potential to make connections with professors, administrators, and the entire outside community. These activities can become virtual minibusinesses as can fund-raising events, homecomings, and alumni weeks.

A group of students interested in studying business might start an investment club or a small enterprise, creating the perfect chance to seek out professors as advisors. In this way they can learn both how to relate and how to perform. At this very moment, all over the United States, students are playing the stock market, catering parties, publishing neighborhood guides, moving other students out of and into apartments. Remember, college is a laboratory, and within it are an extraordinary variety of opportunities for experiments of all kinds. And many professors, counselors, and administrators are willing to act as coaches.

All of these activities also offer chances to find out what you like and what you don't like, what you need to learn and what you already know. If you discover you care more about creating and selling the concept by yourself than you do working together with a team, you might lean toward entrepreneurship rather than a large corporate business environment. But only by experimenting with different roles and settings can you find clues toward answering that most perplexing of questions: "What am I going to do when I finish college?"

Career Qs

Q. Does going for my degree guarantee me work in my profession?

A. There are, alas, no guarantees for anything in life except one. The only thing to do is to live—and live vigorously. Don't just sit in class, waiting to pass, then to graduate. Waiting makes you passive and being passive makes you invisible. Instead, make college your own laboratory for exploring who you are. But know that for the first time in history, one hundred percent of all college graduates have increased chances at success.

USING PREPROFESSIONAL ASSOCIATIONS

Many professional associations offer student memberships and sponsor and support professional clubs for students majoring in the field—engineers, nurses, dentists, teachers, and more. Getting to know professionals in the field is an invaluable source of contacts. The possibility of participation in regional and national conventions afford you a chance to see who's who in the profession as well as to keep abreast of the latest technical developments or trends in the field.

A group of engineering students held a preprofessional seminar just before their national convention. I was invited to conduct a workshop for the students. One of the engineering students was particularly interesting to me because of her questions and ideas. Then during the national convention, I invited her to accompany me to appropriate meetings and meals. As a result, her own charisma became evident to some of the practicing engineers. One of them took an interest in her and helped her obtain employment in a chemical division of a large manufacturing company.

As a side benefit, she has kept me apprised of her subsequent movement and success. I have enjoyed her every letter and call. Professionals and student sponsors all share this same sense of joy from watching a student take risks and grow. And these actions, in turn, embolden all of us to take more chances in our own lives and to encourage our friends, colleagues, and families to do the same.

LEADERSHIP LESSONS

The political arena of student government represents another major area for volunteer activity. Successful people who have entered a race for student office, regardless of whether or not they win, agree that the experience was more worthwhile than they could have dreamed. First, they learned to risk their own egos. It takes courage to lay your ideas on the line and set yourself up for criticism and possible defeat, which is what you do when you run for office.

Secondly, they learned how to create a team of their supporters. It takes courage to ask people not only for their vote, but also to campaign for you. Third, it teaches you to be there when the votes are counted. If you don't win, you have to learn to be a gracious loser, congratulating your opponent and offering him or her your support. If you do win, then you must begin to act on your campaign promises. Winning is an honor, but it is not an end in itself; it is another beginning, a real chance to push forward and make things happen.

"Coming through" is a skill in itself to be practiced, tested, and realized. But it isn't enough. Leadership includes public speaking, demanding that you learn to be able to think on your feet. It requires developing expertise in motivating others, redirecting functions or events, and experience in striking compromises between opposing factions. Only with hands-on practice and experience can you understand the difficult art and process of leadership.

In assuming leadership roles in most student organizations, you have the privilege of working under the direction of a sponsor who is usually someone savvy, wise, and connected. You can expect to have access to professors, administration, alumni, other club presidents, and the outside world in a much broader scope and with greater ease than others might have.

Involvement in student government can, for example, lead to the larger political world. It can start with volunteer work on a politician's campaign, move up to clerkships or internships, even graduate school. It is no accident that many top executives, professionals, and community leaders were political leaders as college and graduate students. Ability to lead is the hallmark of the achiever. The skill that it takes can be developed, nurtured, and made a part of a person's repertoire. Leadership and leadership roles are integrated into the social fabric of our society. We've been talking about getting top roles to practice leadership. But running for office or chairing a committee is not the only way. Learning how to support that designated leader is a critical skill and naturally precedes the actual taking of power.

Steve's Story: A Capitol Decision

Here's a good illustration of how involvement in student activities can help you find a direction.

> Steve had been a student body president, from junior to senior high school, from junior college to Cal State University at Northridge. After spending one year at Cal State without political involvement, he decided to live on campus and run for office, although it would add another year to his program. The mayor, hearing one of his speeches, was impressed enough to invite him to intern with his staff. Continuing to prove himself again on that internship, Steve won a senate fellowship, serving on the senate staff in Sacramento, learning how a bill makes it through and how lobbyists influence that process. These experiences made their mark. He discovered that his calling lies in public service.

If your own goal is to be the leader, you'll learn how to play out that role more effectively by assisting a leader first. Or, if your goal is to be a good team player—there are infinitely more chances for this—you'll get practice sessions. Remember that a supportive role is not a passive one. You don't give up the human trait of "acting" for one of only reacting. Rather, you learn that nobody makes it alone without support—from game planning to morale building. Being supportive requires tremendous attention to the goals and behavior of the leader, to be sure, but also to the group and the outside arena—the rest of the college.

THE MAKING OF WOMEN LEADERS

Recently a group of women who had graduated from Harvard in the '50s got together to pressure the current president of their alma mater. At Harvard, still, as at most Ivy League universities, only a small percent of the tenured faculty are women. Angered at such paltry progress, this group put their money in a trust fund, stipulating that it was not to be spent until more women were hired and promoted. They also swore that they would prevent their grandchildren from attending until equity was established.

Of course, these women hadn't really gone to Harvard, because Harvard in the '50s matriculated only men. These women actually went to Radcliffe, its sister college. Many women found that Radcliffe, like other women's colleges, proved to be a safe haven to practice leadership skills.

Career Qs

Q. As a female student, I am told that I will have a hard time earning the same salary as a comparable male when I graduate. Is this true?

A. Unfortunately, life is still not fair. Although women's salaries have come up a great deal, they are still at least twenty-six percent behind men's. Having a college degree is the single most important factor to higher wages. Even though the glass ceiling is still only cracked for now, it promises to break open early in the 21st century. But for the record, women entrepreneurs and professionals have more of a chance to earn as much as they want to. In these self-motivated ventures, women not only match but often exceed men's accomplishments and earning by one third, according to the National Association of Women Business Owners (NAWBO). There's a long list of impressive women's career and life stories to motivate and inspire you.

Is there ever equality for women, from college on up? The answer is: Keep moving. It's happening. It takes several generations to see real progress. The reality is that we women are still viewed in supporting, not yet leadership roles. Old habits of thought and culture die hard. The problem is that change is resisted hard—even by those of us who want it most. The Department of Labor predicts that women will be filling two-thirds of all newly created jobs in the early part of the 21st century.

Who's the Boss?

As a management consultant to large organizations, part of my work has been to train employees to be more proactive and productive. I have designed problem-solving exercises to develop such initiative and leadership skills. In one such exercise, I divided the participants into small groups, without naming group leaders. Then I gave them the assignment of working in their groups to find the best solution to a hypothetical management problem. The assignment was a mask; the real task lay in uncovering the process.

When the groups finished the assignment, I moved on to the real point of the exercise. I asked the person who had emerged as the leader of each group to stand up.

Without exception, here is what happens: When the group is all male, one man will stand immediately. When I ask why he believes that he was the leader, he answers with a description of what every leader does: He initiated the discussion, took notes, shaped the format, focused the discussion when there were too many tangents, facilitated group participation, summarized the decisions, and accomplished the task within a given time.

The same thing happens when a male is a leader in a mixed (both sexes) group. He stands up immediately, no guessing about it, and recites the same litany of leadership roles.

But when the leader of a mixed group is a woman, she is usually reluctant to stand up in the first place and needs the active encouragement of her group to claim her leadership role. It's as if she can't acknowledege her own power without her group's permission. So, when she does admit that she acted as the leader, she recites the very same activities as her male counterparts. It turns out that leadership is leadership. Its traits are known and recognized. The only difference between genders is the woman's reluctance to claim the title.

But what about all-female groups? Invariably, one of the women says that there was no one leader and claims that the entire group participated equally. This is what people say every time. But when I ask who has taken the responsibility for facilitating, guiding, redirecting, focusing the group, one woman—

usually the one who originally declared that there was no one leader—will finally stand.

This is an amazing process with definite patterns. There are few differences in the way men and women describe their leadership qualities. So it isn't that women are less qualified to be leaders than men, for the simple fact is that as leaders, they perform the very same leaderlike acts. The major difference lies not only in male reluctance to accept women as leaders, but also in women having a harder time, socially and psychologically, to accept themselves as leaders.

If you're a female student, you'll especially need to learn something else besides your academic subjects: confidence in yourself. Confidence to:

- Try difficult subjects and insist on belonging in them
- Speak up in class rather than wait for the safer one-on-one discussion after class
- Debate with authority
- Resist being interrupted or engaging in self-censorship
- Write a paper without feeling cut off from your own thoughts
- Build respect and encouragement from your professors
- Not depend on your physical attractiveness to save you
- Not fear sexual harassment
- Not have to prove yourself over and over

Let's look at what "proving" yourself means. At the bottom of most sexual harassment is expectation. Our society expects young men to do well in college and in their careers. And they usually do. In fact, they have to really mess up to get expelled or fired.

On the other hand, our society doesn't expect the same of women; in fact, it simply doesn't expect women to do well at all. They are excluded from that kind of automatic belonging. To become accepted and valued as more than just competent, therefore, women have to keep proving that they can do it, over and over, each time.

And, in fact, we have come a long way. That glass ceiling keeping women out of top management has been cracked a little but there's so much further to go. Numbers provide the surest measure of women's progress. You can count either by percentage of women represented in various fields or by their salaries.

The median income for men with advanced degrees is
$63,575; women with advanced degrees earn $37,056.
The median income for male doctors is $139,000; for
women doctors, $85,000; male lawyers earn $70,000
while women lawyers average only $52,300.
Source: Worth, March 1997

Is this difference fair? Of course not. Its toll is the shattering of self-image. The issue of confidence sometimes gets lost in a chicken-and-egg issue: Which came first? Ultimately the cause doesn't matter: We have to change our destiny by changing ourselves, inside out. To overcome our own reluctance, therefore, we have to look for specific opportunities to practice living. Some call it leadership. Some call it personal mastery. Some call it life. But it won't change only by law or by itself; we have to keep making ourselves more able.

STRATEGIES TO LEARN ESSENTIAL SKILLS THAT AREN'T TAUGHT IN CLASS

Engage in extracurricular activities and clubs. Start by joining a committee. Up your involvement by running for office. You'll demonstrate initiative, learn to develop people skills (i.e., motivating others, resolving conflicts, solving problems). You'll build leadership skills which involve knowing how to be a team player as well as a star. You'll make and take your rightful place.

Ralph Waldo Emerson's definition of success:

To laugh often and love much, to win the respect of intelligent
persons and the affection of children; to appreciate beauty;
to find the best in others; to give one's self; to leave the world
a lot better whether by a healthy child, a garden patch, or a
redeemed social condition; to have played and laughed with
enthusiasm and sung with exaltation, to know even one life
has breathed easier because you have lived—
this is to have succeeded.

Chapter Six

Real-World Experiments: Internships, Working, Service Learning, and Volunteering

Life's most urgent question is, "What are you doing for others?"
—Martin Luther King Jr.

I wish I could require every student in every major to become involved in as many internships, volunteer activities, and work experiences as possible before graduating. Whatever form it takes and whether it's on or off campus, paid or unpaid, work teaches valuable lessons. Through these activities which run the gamut of doing for others to doing for yourself, you learn about being a world citizen, being mindful of neighbors, joining the community to change what's wrong, sampling the good work of others, defining and finding yourself.

Through these activities which you yourself choose you can learn about where your family has come from, who you are now, and who you want to be. You learn this very often in comparison with others who have very different experiences and backgrounds. Never before has a college campus been such a microcosm of the whole world with foreign students, those who have emigrated here with their families, and those from difference races, religions, economic backgrounds—all with different ideas and values and histories. College is often your first chance to find friends from a more diverse student body than you could have ever imagined. And you will surprise yourself with whom you come to care about through working together in a soup kitchen, a cancer walk, a work-study assignment in the student activities office or interning together for a biotech company.

Make yourself search out these opportunities, sample them, and sign up. You may find, as so many other students have revealed, that through these so-called extracurricular experiences that college takes on new meaning.

INTERNSHIPS

Internships are a real-world, practical complement to classroom theory. Going outside of college, whether you're paid for it or not, provides a great perspective to find out more about what exists in the world as well as more about what exists inside you. Taking the chance to make the match between your talents and your interests in the real world is one of the challenges of college. This kind of opportunity lets you learn more about an industry, company, special interest or cause to help you determine how and where to start your careering process.

Some internships offer a salary; some don't. But even if you don't get paid, you'll have a chance to experience an organization first-hand, test whether you enjoy its work, possibly find a "home" for yourself, and if so, land a job offer.

Typically short-term, internships usually begin with fairly menial tasks within an organization. You are often assigned to be a gofer, running errands and performing small necessary tasks for anyone who needs something done. Or sometimes you are assigned to assist one person who might be working on one special project. Either way, both these kinds of assignments have their advantages.

Being assigned at large lets you see, albeit superficially, a lot more of what goes on within the organization. This general shotgun approach opens doors for you to make connections with any number of people. It's the equivalent of "mailroom" duty for a talent agency, television network or movie studio. You must notice who does what, and what interests you. Then it's up to you to make yourself known, liked, and appreciated by offering help above and beyond your assignment. Your future steps depend on the links you forge. This test of attitude is so powerfully necessary that a few studios have set a policy of limiting their investments in inexperienced people. They will hire you for the mailroom for only six months with the proviso that if you can't make a connection inside in that period of time, you're not suited to work which is so heavily dependent on transactional behavior. Other kinds of businesses don't hire through the mailroom. Accounting firms for example, find a better investment in hiring experienced accountants than going through the expense of training inexperienced men and women who may turn out to be unsuited to the firm.

On the other hand, landing a specific assignment gives you direct experience in learning the difficulties and rewards of working together with a team. You become better known to the people you work with because the group is smaller. Either way, students report that internships are the very best way to find out what goes on, test whether it's for you or not, then if it is for you, get the edge on a potential job, or if it's not, change directions.

Internships aren't new. In fact, the oldest and most traditional internship program began in medicine, where year-long internships, often in other cities or states, immediately after four years of medical study are prerequisites to becoming licensed in the field. In law school, students usually take summer internships with firms which they hope to join between their second and third years. Law students aggressive enough to acquire such internships are usually offered positions with their respective law firms following graduation. Some law grads go on to clerk for judges in a more formal system of internships. Education has a long history of requiring student teaching, which is helpful both to practice what you've been preparing for as well as finally judge whether your choice is still appropriate for you.

More business organizations are now offering internships to students as a sure way to identify potential talent and to establish a reservoir of qualified future employees. They look for a bonus as well—students bringing the latest academic theory and technology to the company.

Southern California's number-one industry, entertainment, is hard to crack without prior access. Internships have become the main means of opening the door to such opportunities. Radio and television networks as well as record companies are now participating in internships for college and university students who major in communication, cinema, arts, and journalism. Just as you would hope, these internships are quite different from the structured curricula of the classroom. Students as interns learn to pitch in and go the extra mile in a work environment with intense daily pressures and chaotic work schedules.

The University of Cincinnati, Ohio's Antioch, and Philadelphia's Drexel University have pioneered in work-study programs in which a paid job in the student's area of study is a part of the academic curriculum. Students can get credit for a semester or a full year for working. Smith College's model internship program offers hundreds of opportunities for their liberal arts undergraduate women. Californian colleges and universities have participated in the Educational Participation in Communities Program (EPIC) which offers students real-life work experience as a means of developing job skills and exploring career options while at the same time helping solve problems in the community. Internships continue to grow in number and in opportunity.

Survey Responses: How Did You Choose?

*In our "Undergrad-itudes" survey, we asked the question,
"How did you decide which college to attend?" Here's how the
respondents answered.*

Response	Number of people
Reasonably priced	147
Best in Field	117
Quality of Life	104
Closest to home	92
Went with friends	18
Only acceptance	6

If your college career center doesn't have an internship program or if you can't find one that you like, ask a counselor to help. Don't be stopped. You can always initiate your own internship. Here's how:

- Find an organization for which you think you'd like to work.

- Decide which department you'd like to work in, or plan to rotate in a few different ones to learn which you prefer.

- Call the department(s) you're interested in and offer yourself as an intern even if they don't have an established program.

If you need more assistance, see your career counselor. And ask your professors who are often consultants to companies within the areas of your interests and are likely to have direct contacts and large networks of associates to get you started. It's then up to you to thank them and to find a way to stay in contact with them, giving regular progress reports and asking for advice. This establishes a healthy mentor-protégé role

Using Internships as Direction Finders

If you really don't have a clear notion of what you want to do following graduation, you're not alone. More students than ever before don't! If you are looking for direction, an internship can help clarify your uncertainties and focus your interests. Which organizations should you consider? The answer, of course, is all kinds—newspapers, hospitals, radio and television stations, emergency help centers, political organizations, religious groups, retail stores, import-export businesses, libraries, schools, advertising and public relations agencies, factories, labor unions, financial firms—in short, all kinds of small and large businesses, arts, services, and professions. Choose the one closest to your own interests and course of study and go exploring.

Career Qs

Q.When is the best time to get an internship?

A. Your sophomore year is not too early to start planning for an internship. It's essential for every junior and senior to have at least one a year. Internships let you test out the field you think you want. If it works, then you can start creating a network of experts and mentors, and get the job offer you want. If it doesn't work, you have time to explore other options before you graduate. At the least, it's fail-safe; at the most, it's an entrée into your dream job.

You are actually engaged in a quest to find your direction. You want to discover places and opportunities to find and develop your talents and aptitudes. Or, if you have not been able to identify a goal and feel unable to define what it is you want to do, then start experimenting with work. Start anywhere and look for those aspects that interest you more than others. Don't worry: You'll find something that you'll like enough to build on. We discover how to match our talents to our interests in a variety of different ways that we'd never expect.

Sara's Story: A Volunteer Finds a Home

We don't always know what we're interested in. Interests need to be uncovered and explored. Here's a story of a student who used an internship to explore an area that she didn't know much about that had piqued her curiosity.

To pay for her tuition, Sara, an environmental geography major, worked part time in her university's law library. Without any passion for either her courses or her work, Sara was sleep-walking in some kind of limbo that too many of us endure. Early in her junior year, Sara decided to try an internship in an area she had just read about with interest. At the city planning coun-cil, Sara discovered to her joy that she had "come home," experiencing her first sense of belonging. She then redirected her major and threw herself into her studies while taking on more work at the council. Not only did Sara create her own internship, she began the more significant task of reshaping her-self.

Realize that Sara didn't just walk in and get assigned to the most interesting project with the most visibility. Not by a long shot. Initially, she performed menial "gofer" tasks: answering phones, stuffing envelopes, clipping newspaper stories, proof-reading papers, and so on. She had to learn to forgo her ego, be consistently cheerful, and willing, even eager, to perform without complaint these inherently boring tasks for the chance at being in this profession.

In addition to her involvement in her work, she had a chance to advance in her course of study and gain perspective on how an office actually works. She also had the unique advantage of seeing role models and possibilities right under her nose. Here she was, part of things, working alongside some of the people she most admired on projects she was becoming fasci-nated with. She took the time to ask the planners about their career stories and personal goals—how they began, and why they continued. What could be more rewarding and worth the risk?

As college students, how do we make our first career choices? Too often we are programmed to pursue what is currently in vogue. You can often tell the decade in which people went to college by their majors. Looking back, we see that in the '50s, males were sent to college to become engineers; females studied to be teachers. In the '60s—if they hadn't dropped out—males studied community service or psychology, while females pursued social work or sociology. In the '70s, males went to computer science or law school; females began to study law or entered M.B.A. programs in significant numbers. By the '80s, business became the most commonly chosen major for both genders. And in the '90s, the most commonly chosen major turned out to be communications.

We can't escape the fact that we as individuals live among trends. The dilemma has always been to choose wisely, yet personally among so wide a range of choices. There's a heavy cost in not figuring your own desires into the career equation. Too many of us come out of school unstimulated, dissatisfied, and still undecided about what to do with our degrees because our choices weren't based on our own personal strengths and interests. Where do we discover information about how to choose our life's work? T.V. shows and movies feed us caricatured images of medicine, law, media, and police work, and this is all we know about many jobs.

You are expected to choose a career without having much experience to draw upon. Like that old line about understanding modern art, we expect the same of our best career choice—that we will "know it when we see it." We can't usually pull the label of a career out of thin air, even if we do recognize our own talents and preferences. But what we can do is use our time in college to experiment with ideas and possibilities—courses, professors, internships, and jobs, to find our callings, the work we're best suited to do.

Career Qs

Q. I'm an engineering student and don't know whether to switch to business to get a better job after graduation.

A. *Here's how to make yourself more marketable and valuable:*

- *Instead of switching majors at the last moment, add a few business courses.*

- *Get two internships: one at an engineering firm, the other at a smaller or more entrepreneurial firm. Then talk to a career counselor or a professor about choosing a direction after you've had hands-on experience.*

- *Interview successful engineers (at internship sites and through professors' recommendations) who left the technical track for the managerial one and ask what they'd recommend.*

Don't choose before you have information and real experience; don't decide alone.

Some words of comfort: People who don't know what it is they want to do are not stupid. The Higher Education Research Institute at U.C.L.A. found differences between those female students who came to college with preset career goals and majors, and those who were undecided. The undecided students tested out to be more intelligent and flexible, finally making appropriate choices after a process of trial and error.

Intern #1: Fine Tuning

An internship gives you the chance to test your dreams. In this first story, an intern found a career that suited him even better than the dream job he originally imagined.

> From the first time he listened to music on the radio, Gary had wanted to be a disc jockey. It seemed to him that deejays were powerful and had simply the best job in the world. His dreams came true in college when he landed an internship with a local radio station show that played Top 40 hits. As an intern, he was required to do a variety of tasks that were quite different from the job of deejay: delivering the mail, running errands, helping on a promotion campaign, and finally substituting for a vacationing salesperson. He discovered, to his astonishment, not only that these other jobs were significant, but that marketing and sales were his real talents. Redirecting his childhood dream, he developed a successful career in media marketing. Taking the risk of interning at a radio station, Gary learned about areas that he would not have thought of before. This internship was his "direction finder." Today he is the president of a major network.

Intern #2: Shifting Gears

Here's another kind of internship experience, one that reveals how wrong a career choice can be.

> Richard had always wanted to be a teacher; near the end of his college program, he signed up for student teaching, the traditional internship in the education field. He was assigned to teach history in a public high school. Midway through the semester, Richard realized that he had made a bad choice for himself. It was history that he loved, not the actual teaching process. He didn't have enough patience for his students; he disliked the slow pace of teaching; and he felt constrained by the restrictions in text selection. At the end of student teaching, he promptly shifted gears.
>
> Richard found another internship at the city newspaper. Because of his teaching experience, his proposal for a special series on education was accepted. During his time at the paper, he sought out news reporters for advice and was hired by one of those reporters, who had, in turn, been promoted to editor. Two attempts gave Richard the chance to know himself more clearly so that he could identify his own interests and style. His courage to change served him in the very best way.

Intern #3: Psych Experiment Pays Off

Another story about second thoughts belongs to Lisa.

> Lisa had chosen psychology as an undergraduate major but was devastated when her classroom theory didn't match her fantasy of the drama of psychotherapy. As a last chance to test herself before she changed majors, Lisa interned at a local crisis clinic taking incoming calls on the hotline. After she proved herself able, she was then invited to assist a group counselor, and finally trained to be a lay therapist. By the time she graduated, she had a caseload of her own clients. Lisa's internship served to affirm her original choice and saved her career. This inter-

vention also taught her about the nature of experimenting. She is a much better therapist as well as supervisor now than she would ever have been without the experience of the internship.

Some colleges are trying to forge the connection between their students and alumni with the same career interests. Through the shared career experiences and professional insights over lunch or dinner, the students get an up-close, personal view of a profession, warts and all, in order to check out their assumptions, whet their appetites, and possibly allow them to sort out previously held choices or decide to pursue others. Be sure to find out about and sign up for these activities.

Be Someone Else for a Day

I managed a brilliantly conceived conference whose purpose was to do just that kind of career reality check. Called "Alternative Pursuits to America's Third Century," the conference helped participants, who came from all walks of life from all over the United States, plan and implement their own community service. But before they could create an original design, they had to "be someone else for a day." This exercise required conferees to pick several careers that interested them, no matter how unrealistic these choices were. Then they had to find people who worked in those fields, follow them around, and observe closely what they actually did during the course of a full day.

Imagine what field you'd choose, how you get yourself in to be a "fly on the wall," and how your observations would match your fantasies.

This experiment overwhelmingly shattered these participants' illusions. I remember one psychologist who had thought that investigative reporting would be the most stimulating job imaginable. Feeling his own career choice too safe and slow in delivering results, he found to his amazement that the actual work of tracking down clues was a completely boring and ultimately unrewarding process. Able to reassess what he was doing, he revised his advice to his own patients, reflecting what he had learned about the dangers of defining one's vocation from fantasy without checking it out first. He became far more stimulated and interested in finding the keys to his patients' dilemmas. Reading mysteries, however, remained high on his list of hobbies, puzzles that simultaneously provided insight into and an escape from his practice.

Another participant, a social worker, took the opposite route and chose what she thought was the worst occupation—waitressing. Going to a local diner to observe the waitress's routine, she discovered that her subject did much more than just take orders and bring on the eggs. Under close observation, the waitress turned out to be an on-the-spot social worker, joking easily with regular customers, asking about their lives, sympathizing with their problems, and celebrating their progress. It was a revelation to this professional woman, who had considered her own job as the ultimate in the helping profession. She came away with a completely new perspective on the social nature of work.

Internship Dos and Don'ts

An internship can offer many rich opportunities. But don't expect miracles. Don't complain if you feel that your assigned task is beneath you, if you aren't appreciated, if the work is too complicated for a minimal (or nonexistent) wage, or if the assignment is too short or chaotic or meaningless. And when your assigned work isn't going well, don't ignore it or try to fudge it, or wait for someone to come rescue you. Ask for help from your supervisor. You are not supposed to know the ropes, but you are expected to be honest and responsible. Getting advice when you need it is part of the job.

So take it as it comes. Be enthusiastic, friendly, and ready to help. Make friends. Don't take obvious sides in office politics which can swamp you. Save your personal questions for casual, off-work times, such as lunch or breaks. Don't ask for career advice too often (like every day) from your co-workers. But do ask which courses might provide good background for your field, which to forget, how to gain entry to your chosen career, and finally, what to consider in choosing a career. Ask your supervisors for stories about their professional experiences, so that you can gain insight into the nature of this kind of work. When you don't know what to do next, ask. You'll not only be learning how to get along with people in an office situation, but you'll also be increasing your awareness of your field. Such an opportunity can turn the job into the beneficial experience it could be.

Career Qs

Q. I'm a speech communication major graduating in May. I had a great internship experience at a small public relations firm. I would like to continue to work for them full time after graduation. The company would like to keep me, but they have no

openings right now. Should I wait until something opens up or start looking for another job?

A. Even though you feel comfortable with your company, you just can't afford to wait for two reasons:

(1) They might not hire anyone for a year (a financially unbearable).

(2) If you stay with this employer, you'll never know how valuable you are to others.

Stay in touch with the company so you aren't forgotten whenever an opportunity opens. But in the meantime, start networking like crazy. Go out interviewing for jobs, using your internship experience to launch you in the workforce. You may just find something even better with a company who'd fight to have you! It takes courage—inner resources—to realize the value of what you've learned. For tips on the job search process, sign up for a workshop at your career center.

Internship Strategies

Try out internships.

Sign up for one each semester—you can find them at the career center. Or create them for yourself. Internships give you an entrée to the worlds you may want, or let you explore ones you secretly desire. Hint: Don't expect organizations to give you some version of a course outline. The real world doesn't work that way. Instead, do everything they ask and more. Snoop. Find out what people are doing. Offer your assistance, and you'll be included.

Act like a talk show host in your daily life: Interview everyone you meet.

Imagine you've got your own talk show, and everyone is your guest: faculty, school staff, co-workers and bosses. Ask a lot of questions. As a talk show host, your script might include a list of questions like these.

How did you get started?

What do you like about your job?

What's the hardest part of your job?

What kind of help did you get along the way?

How did you get this job?

What advice do you have for me?

By the way, don't worry about being a pest; people love to talk about themselves.

WORKING YOUR WAY THROUGH

Work is less boring than amusing oneself.
—Charles Baudelaire

Work in any form offers extraordinary possibilities to further your education, experimentation, connection, and yes, even profit. This is true whether it's on campus or off, full time or part time, work-study, a paid or unpaid internship. The only drawback: Work is time-consuming and energy draining. You'll have to develop your time-management skills and budget how you spend your time for studying as well as for socializing. You'll be left with zip time for goofing off. But that is the worst handicap.

Here are the ten best reasons to work:

- Work provides active and hands-on experience, often a welcome change from sitting in class taking notes.

- Work relieves your battered ego as you switch roles from anxious test taker to eager doer. (This is particularly true for older, returning students who are accustomed to autonomy and responsibility.)

- A job helps confirm a career decision and speeds you on to get hired or have a stepping stone.

- Or, by showing you where you chose wrong, it can act as a catalyst to redirect you.

- Work furnishes a laboratory in which to test theories learned in class; it also presents situations in which to practice solving real problems.

- Work offers opportunities to bring experiences to bear on classroom work, thereby enriching it.

- Work helps develop the critical interpersonal skills of communication and collaboration.

- Work helps pay for tuition and living expenses.

- Ultimately, work serves as a bridge for the transition between college and career.

- Not working is not an inspiring alternative.

If you're smart and lucky, you can match your interests to the work you choose. It's worth every sacrifice to find that right work. If, say, you're interested in the entertainment field, which traditionally, alas, does not pay its interns, go after that unpaid internship anyway to gain the necessary entrance to that industry—even if it means having to take a paying job at night or over the weekends.

Work serves more than one purpose. You can achieve all these benefits if you use work for more than just earning money. Students who work at part-time or summer jobs just to pay expenses often live in a double world: work versus college. This is a tough dichotomy that too often translates into *work versus life* once students graduate and find jobs. To make both work and life better, look for jobs that interest and expand you or find a way to expand a dull job to make it more interesting.

For example, a district attorney who had never lost a case told me a story from his past, a story that became a touchstone for his later success. To supplement a partial college scholarship, he worked as a salesclerk in a department store. Bored, he decided to experiment to see if he could differentiate those customers who would buy something from those who were just browsing. When he perfected this skill, he stepped up his experiment. He then tried to sell to the non-buyers. In the process, he taught himself the psychology of sales, motivation, and persuasion—skills that he developed as a trial lawyer, successfully winning over to his side every judge and jury that he stood before.

Think of it. Whether you work in a jeans store or fast-food chain, the university's fund-raising office or sales department in a T.V. station—you have a rich experimental field before you. It is ripe for anything you want to study or have been assigned. Our district attorney could have continued his experiment and written up his findings for papers in psychology or marketing or business courses as well as in the campus newspaper, a marketing journal, or even the local newspaper's business section. What he learned enriched and emboldened him—and it paid for his living expenses.

The Making of a Doctor and an Entrepreneur

A well-known doctor has created a business that has revolutionized the way health information is delivered. He was one of the first doctors to use television to bring positive information about cancer prevention and cures to the public. Later, he broadened his discussion to cover any issues affecting illness and health. He has also started his own health cable network and written books and produced audiotapes. Through these various media, he attempts to promote our responsibility for our well being. But he wasn't born into this unusual medical career.

While he was an undergrad at U.C.L.A., he started two competing day camps to fund his medical school training. He hired his athletic fraternity brothers as camp counselors; the camps were so successful that they still exist today. You can see the thread that runs through the doctor's career. Early on, he earned a living by providing a health-promoting service. In this way he brought entrepreneurial skills to the medical profession.

John J-H Kim's Story

John J-H Kim recently sold his successful minority career fair and publishing business, Crimson & Brown Associates, to Kaplan, and he joined Kaplan to expand the job fair business. John has been honing his entrepreneurial skills ever since he was a child selling stationery door-to-door. At Phillips Academy, he started one of the largest student clubs and organized the Asian Student Union, recruiting speakers from his active fund-raising efforts. Later, at Brown, he continued his support of Asian American students. To finance his last two years at Harvard, he worked as a sales assistant for IBM's PC fairs, learning the art and business of conducting business fairs from the masters of business enterprises themselves.

After a summer internship at Procter and Gamble, he went to work for McKinsey & and Company to take advantage of its famous business training. In one year, when he was only 22, the company gave him the responsibility of making presentations to a five-billion-dollar German company in Hong Kong for his company. Building on his skills as salesman, instigator, leader, and businessman, John brought this expertise to the still-unmet needs of minority students, his dedicated concern, and began his own company with two of his college friends as partners.

At the same time, he enrolled in Harvard's M.B.A. program and used Crimson & Brown as his case study, taking it to great success. Putting both his passions and skills to work, he created a niche that also helps so many others.

"It's totally up to you," he attests. "No one is going to do it for you, but if you take the initiative, your momentum will carry a lot of other people along with you. That's a lesson that will stay with me as I go through life."

If you recognize your own entrepreneurial interests, plan on starting your own business while you are in college. You'll develop skills to build on and you'll make so much more than just an hourly rate. Like the entrepreneurial doctor and John J-H Kim, start with your own interests and skills, even passions. If you haven't identified them yet, think about what you do in your free time, what you notice when you shop, what you read for pleasure, where you like to spend time or browse, whom you admire, what groups you'd like to belong to. Survey what's needed and possible. Let your imagination wander anywhere: from catering and delivering food to students, to investing in the stock market.

Career Qs

Q. How do I ethically respond to an offer of a part-time job now in my senior year when my real goal is full-time work after graduation?

A. First, know that you don't ever have to reveal your own ultimate goals to anyone. After all, no employer reveals its ultimate goals to its employees. As students we're used to telling the whole "truth," but we're not taught self-protection. Take a lesson. And, take that part-time job for now. Who knows; an opportunity might emerge on the job that convinces you to stay on. But if not, it's okay to give notice after you've graduated and landed a fine, full-time position. In fact, it is acceptable work behavior. The work world is unlike college: There are no contracts, even implicit ones, for long-term, let alone part-time employment.

Your goals in the work world will be (1) doing the best work you can and (2) developing the best relationships with management where you are for however long you remain. That best leads to more success—both within yourself and in the world.

SERVICE LEARNING

The best part of the '60s has returned, just in a new format. Altruism is back where it belongs, starting in college. On campuses everywhere, from Penn to Vanderbilt to Alverno, students are again feeling the impulse to learn from and improve society by rolling up their sleeves to help communities in need. Service Learning is the new name for this involvement. It falls between volunteering with no obligations, and interning in an organization, primarily for career or financial goals. Service Learning lets you earn academic credit for providing a semester's assistance to a community service organization. You have to register for service learning classes or sign up for special projects. You're usually required to write up the valuable insights or lessons you've learned in a journal or term paper. This can often be your personal reflections on the experience of performing service work right in the middle of the community at its neediest.

Interested in helping low-earners struggle to figure out their taxes? Determining which services actually reach the neediest cases? Assisting juveniles to bypass further hassles in court and get on with the process of building healthy lives? Projects like these exist— if your professors are willing to design and facilitate them, launch you into agencies, and then help you evaluate what you've found. Besides getting credit, you learn so much about the relationship between dire need and appropriate assistance. You will be taking the time to investigate how our society works from the inside out—combining academic theory with real world application. Who'll benefit? You most of all—no matter if you are majoring in social sciences, computer science, engineering, accounting, or the humanities; in other words: any academic pursuit.

Service learning is not available on every campus, but it's slowly making headway. It's gaining momentum now as federal funding dovetails with academic interest in creating educated citizens. If a service learning program doesn't exist at your school, persuade a professor to create such a project for your class, or an independent study just for you.

VOLUNTEERING

Volunteering is the American conscience. According to *USA Today* "Snapshots" from April 1997, the Pew Research Center lists the good deeds being done every day and has found that people in the United States volunteer their time and help shape their nation in the following ways:

Church/religious group	38%
Poor/elderly/homeless aid	34%
Youth groups (scouts, etcetera)	26%
Neighborhood/community group	23%
School/tutoring program	22%
Hospital/health organization	11%
Environmental group	11%
Political candidate/party	8%

It's more than just doing good deeds. Volunteers are willing to take action to build and rebuild the communities they want to live in—schools, libraries, parks, museums, hospitals, food banks, city government, or just talking to a kid in trouble. What you do is far greater than only giving aid to someone in need. Volunteering is about your participation in creating a society that you want to live in. It increases your senses of belonging and community spirit.

You can sign up for one-day events (an AIDS Walk), weekends spent rebuilding houses (Habitat for Humanity), or create a program around your own schedule. Los Angeles, for example, has 40,000 nonprofit organizations eager to include you, no matter how skilled or nonskilled you are. Some city and county agencies will cover your transportation and parking costs, even a meal, in return for your time.

Few volunteer programs have galvanized a nation's soul as much as President John Kennedy's internationally focused Peace Corps, still alive since the 1960s. It's often rated as the most significant transformational event in their lives by those who volunteered, learned another language, traveled to third world countries, learned from the people they went to teach, met, befriended, and sometimes married other volunteers.

President Clinton's AmeriCorp, aimed at ending illiteracy within the United States, has invited volunteers to teach reading in elementary schools. Organized volunteer groups exist on nearly every college campus to open a world and to share information particularly for new immigrants who would otherwise not have the language skills for access to it.

Believe it or not, volunteering turns out to be a great bargain. You'll learn a lot about others but mostly, yourself. You'll contribute to your own confidence by discovering that you can be part of something greater than yourself and make a difference. You'll have a great time making friends with other volunteers whom you'd never have had a chance to meet. These benefits can be yours whether you're working on a political campaign or in an animal sanctuary. Finally, you might find inspiration from one activity that will grow into an internship, service learning, or even a career.

Wrap-Up

There's a world of jobs and opportunities available for college students—working on campus through internships, part-time and full-time jobs including work-study jobs, service learning, as well as volunteering. You can locate all these opportunities for jobs, internships, and events from your career center, volunteer center, or student activities center. There are lists in printouts and in computer directories in your career center. You can even connect directly to some of the sponsor organizations yourself through computer links.

It's easy to find work that will change your life. All you have to do is start here and pass go.

Chapter Seven
Discovering Who You Are and What You Want to Do

There's no security in life, only opportunity.
—Mark Twain

You won't skid if you stay in a rut.
—Kin Hubbard

What's the difference between *career* and *success*? They're synonymous. The original meaning of *career* is to *progress through life*. The original meaning of *success* is *one thing after another*, like the succession of presidents. Eureka! *Career* and *success* mean the same thing; both imply movement and growth, rather than a set point or position. These redefinitions of familiar words provide fresh insight about the inevitable choices we face not only at graduation but, for most of us, throughout our lives. And will we ever need the insight to debunk the myths that lead to some distorted expectations.

MYTHS THAT LEAD TO DISTORTED EXPECTATIONS

Here are some of the most common misperceptions that interfere with finding our true directions in life.

Myth #1: Success Means Finding the Right Career

The Department of Labor predicts that most of us will transition through four or five different careers and move within them through as many as fifteen different jobs. In the traditional model, workers traded their lifetime loyalty to a company for job security. The new mobility suggested by the Labor Department statistics demands our taking total responsibility for managing our own careers and our money. The kinds of work—the *What,*—will change along with the marketplace and technology. But the process of finding work—the *How*—remains the same. No matter what kind of work you'll end up doing, finding good work to do will become a skill in itself. You'll have to learn:

- How to reach out and make connections.
- How to take advantage of new opportunities.
- How to develop skills.
- How to build alliances with others

This megaskill of finding meaningful work is at the heart of the expression *being in the right place at the right time.* We are, of course, at some place at any moment; therefore the science of right timing means taking the chance that leads out.

You don't have to go it alone. Learn to use the services and counselors in your career center. And don't do it just because this will help you meet your immediate goals of finding an internship, or landing your first job after graduation. Think of it as developing a strategy that will become key to achieving success throughout your life. The strategy is to build your confidence by connecting with people and ideas to give more, and therefore get more out of life. Make a lifelong habit of getting the help you need from the most appropriate source. And learn to return the favor with thanks and help in kind.

Myth #2: Self-Reliance

If you read the biographies of great people, a great motivator and educator, you'll recognize the connections, negotiations, and risks behind the development of successful people back before they achieved success. You'll learn about the courage they had to connect themselves to others. You'll learn to give up that false god of complete independence. While it's true that you have to initiate your contracts and carry through on what you've promised to do, you won't pull yourself up by your own bootstraps too often. If you think about it, it's a physical impossibility to pull yourself up by your bootstraps unless they're nailed to the ceiling. I hope that while you're in college, you can debunk the bootstrap myth and develop strategies for learning, to risk relationships and collaboration.

Myth #3: You Should Already Know Who You Are and What You Want to Do

More than just an institution from which you can get a degree, college is the place where you can take the chance to shape your fantasies as well as shape yourself in the image of these fantasies. Who we are and what we want to be can be a very definite concept within us, or the seeds of our identity can lie hidden or dormant. For most of us, discovering our talents and finding work that suits us takes a long time. Identifying our dreams is a continuing process in life because we grow and change just as the marketplace does. But the skills we need to cultivate a fantasy and shape it into reality continue to be learned and shaped.

All the proposed activities in the preceding chapters—about actively developing mentor relationships, participation in clubs and activities, involvement in internships and part-time work, using papers and projects for investigation—are strategies to connect you to worlds of interest outside to find what mirrors your own world or inspires you. Through such active engagement in college, you can begin to discover your identity through your interests, skills, passions; the sum total of what we think of as our callings.

USING THE CAREER CENTER

Your college's career center can also help you in the process of finding yourself and taking your first career steps. Most college career centers are resource centers. They usually offer the following services, free or at very low costs.

Top Twelve Reasons to Go to the Career Center

1. For individual and group career counseling by professionals.

2. For career workshops on choosing a career and job searching plus hands-on training in specific tactics such as résumé writing or job interviewing.

3. To take vocational tests that can help you match your interests to career paths by aligning your skills and talents to those of professionals.

4. To browse through the library of books, videotapes, and other career resources.

5. To find internship listings.

6. To check out listings of part-time jobs, on- and off-campus.

7. To check out phone, print, and online listings for full-time jobs.

8. To attend a job fair and meet prospective employers.

9. To attend career conferences to learn the career paths, experiences, and advice from successful people in fields you want to enter as well as those you had never before considered.

10. To make connections with employers.

11. To meet with employers' recruiters on campus.

12. For information and advice on selecting a graduate schools.

Use your college's career center early, even in your sophomore year. Don't wait until the final month before graduation to make your first appointment. Counseling centers regularly offer workshops in all aspects of career planning— from choosing a career and figuring out what you can really do with your major to selecting internships and getting a job.

Career Counselors

Each career center is staffed with a group of professionals called career counselors, whose mission is to help you find yours. They have had training in assessing career choices. They can administer vocational and personality tests. And they can also help you to interpret your scores and make sense of them, if possible. They can also make and share contacts in the business, arts, and service communities both on and off the campus. They are great sources of support and can be powerful allies. They offer career insights, leading you to a variety of sources of career information and direct you to ways to get experience and mentoring. They can assist you in writing your résumé and cover letter, coach you to present yourself to recruiters and other interviewers, and guide you in making your choice and negotiating the best starting offer possible.

But remember that career counselors are people, too. They need to be cultivated. Take the initiative: Make an appointment. Get to know them. Let them get to know about you.

Survey Responses: Friends

In our "Undergrad-itudes" survey, we asked the question, "How have you made friends?" Here's how the respondents answered.

Response	Number of people
In classes	220
In dorm	151
Through clubs	123
From high school	60

STRATEGY: USE YOUR CAREER CENTER EARLY AND OFTEN

Run, don't walk, to your school's career center. Especially if you're ready to graduate. Especially if you're not. Get information and advice. Get tested and see if the results match your own criteria. Sign up for workshops such as job-searching and job interviewing strategies. Don't just sit there: Be active. Participate. Make your college experiences reveal your talents in a kind of personal laboratory, much like developing photographs, gradually revealing an image from a blank piece of paper.

GET TO KNOW YOURSELF

Knowing yourself and being able to describe yourself to other people are critical skills in themselves. I've devised a series of questions that you can ask yourself that will help you in the process. It's a way of brainstorming with yourself to learn who you've been, what you've enjoyed, and what you hope for. But if you don't make an effort to work with yourself to divine some of the answers, you'll always elude yourself. Yet we hope that others will see us better than we can see ourselves. We hope that someone else will be able to explain our talents to us, for us. Sometimes that can really happen through career counselors and vocational assessments. But it helps to have an initial "take" on yourself before you go to the career center. Try working with the "Interview Yourself" exercise at the end of the chapter. Then take the results with you to your career center to help your counselor cut to the chase and help you more accurately.

Career Qs

Q. I'm working part time selling clothes and want to be sure that I don't end up here. I'm a liberal-arts major starting my junior year, and I am getting worried. What's your advice?

A. Don't worry; be happily proactive! But don't be prejudiced against sales. After all, most of us have to persuade others to our point of view, whether we're pitching a screenplay to an editor, detailing the worthiness of a charity to a donor, or proposing a project to a professor or a boss. These are all forms of selling. Without developing self-presentation skills, you won't advance in any career you choose.

If you love people, and love putting people together with ideas, products, services, as well as other people, you'll love selling. Selling also brings in great financial rewards: You can earn anywhere from $35,000 to over $600,000. Reconsider the rich, and usually hidden area of selling in any of these areas—art, education, books, science, computers, shopping centers, cars, yachts, vitamins, movies, people (headhunting), money (investments), insurance, training programs, or clothes. You can sell your service or product any place in the United States or abroad—Scotland, Brazil, Singapore.

Explore a lot more before turning away from something you don't think is intellectual or exciting. There's so much more to it than your experience just selling jeans behind a counter.

Vocational Assessments

Deep down, we all like to take self-assessment tests. We want feedback; we want "real" answers about who we are and what we should be doing. If there are telephone psychics and fortune-tellers, why not a test that reveals and matches our inner desires to our outward skills?

Well, indeed, every center does provide vocational testing for a vast number of students who simply don't know have a clue about they want to do. Many of these tests are available online with immediate scoring and interpretation. There are a variety of interactive computerized career assessments, such as SIGI Plus, FOCUS, the updated Strong (including the Holland typology of 297 occupations). These career assessments have a number of benefits:

- They correlate your likes and dislikes, interests, and values with a databank of thousands of responses by other individuals already in designated occupations

- They help you articulate your priorities and values

- They provide a point of discussion for your career counseling sessions

Take Note

Assessments reveal preferences, but they can't predict changes in your future interests or skills any more than they can predict the marketplace's future. They are limited to matching your interests to the activities of people who perform various types of work known when the test was created.

Interpretation is vital to making sense of the results offered by the tests. Your career counselor is trained to help with this process and to question its relevance and, above all, your reactions.

Career Qs

Q. I want to be involved in the music industry, but I am not really a musician. What are my chances?

A. Here are career paths you can start thinking about

- *music agent*
- *contracts or copyright lawyer for songwriters*
- *publicity agent for a record company*
- *demo tape producer*
- *interactive project manager*
- *advertising copywriter*
- *CD distributor*
- *retail sales*
- *radio or party deejay*
- *classical or popular music critic*
- *music librarian*

- *music teacher*
- *music therapist*
- *college concert promoter*
- *audio engineer*
- *sound systems manufacturer*

Personality Assessments

More accurate than vocational assessments are personality assessments. These can be astonishingly accurate. We love to take them to learn more about ourselves. Oddly enough, we get so little feedback from most of life about who we are, what our personalities are, or how we compare to others. Learning about our style of behavior and basic personality characteristics is interesting, informative, and comforting. One of the most popular, the Myers-Briggs Inventory, for example, is an easy to take, multiple-choice, self-report assessment. The Myers-Briggs Inventory is based on Carl Jung's theory of conscious psychological types to describe your individual mode of information gathering and decision making.

But there are many dilemmas unexplained by any of these assessment instruments. First, each profession is complex, offering many different types of work. That complexity in turn, attracts and promotes different personalities, styles, and motivations. Even though law school curriculum and bar association tests are standardized, every kind of law practice, for example, demands a different personality. Trial lawyers are more dramatic, aggressive, spontaneous; patent lawyers typically lower-key, more research oriented; family law attorneys more psychologically attuned to individual clients; estate lawyers, more financially adept; corporate attorneys, more businesslike; and entertainment lawyers, well, they are often like, and sometimes actually become, celebrities themselves. So, what personality is best suited for a lawyer? Well, it depends . . . .

Secondly, in every decade, one-third of all careers are newly created, according to the Department of Labor. That means these tests need to be constantly updated to include new careers that have been created. And of course, these careers can't be conceived of in advance. Vocational tests obviously can't include career paths that haven't emerged yet. They are based on history, not prediction.

Despite their limitations, however, vocational tests can be a great start to recognize glimmerings of yourself. Think of them as the sieve in a process much like panning for gold. Know that you're not the only one who doesn't know what you want to be or do. Most of us are clueless when it comes to discovering what we really want—or recognizing it when we see it. As a former labor negotiator, I can tell you that the most difficult problem of all is getting people to realize what they really want, not what they think they want or believe that others want for them. Finding yourself is a learned process that comes from activities, experimentation, and evaluation. Take advantage of any tools that can help.

INTERVIEW YOURSELF

Your entry into "real life" begins with an exploration of *yourself.* You are more than the sum of your height, weight, age, grades, work history, and references. You are also your ideas, aspirations, likes and dislikes, fears, interests, predilections, beliefs, and dreams. But we are often blind to these aspects of ourselves.

Work through the following questions to help you:

- Organize your thoughts about yourself
- Categorize what you have done
- Inventory the things you like
- Learn about your philosophy or how you approach life
- Identify what kind of help and information you'd like

Try answering these questions before you visit your career center. The more you can tell career center staff about yourself, and what you want to find out, the better they can help.

My name is

_____

I'm also called

_____

My academic focus is on these fields or subjects

_____

_____

_____

Most frequently my career objective is

_____

_____

What I think I do best

_____

_____

What I do just to please me

_____

_____

What I'd like to do better

_____

_____

What people don't suspect I do well

_____

_____

The things people can usually count on me for are

_____

_____

What I consider most rewarding about a job or activity
(First add any rewards that are important to you that are not on the list, then rank the whole list. Give the most important item a "1," the next most important a "2," and so on.)

_____   Applause

_____   Awards

_____   Compensation

_____   Excitement

_____   Laughs

_____   Praise from peers

_____   Recognition

_____   Self-satisfaction

_____   _____

_____   _____

_____   _____

_____   _____

_____   _____

_____   _____

The things I'd like to get from the career center are

_____

_____

The things I'd like to see added to the career center are

_____

_____

Other possibilities

_____

_____

The music I like

_____

_____

The news I pay attention to is about

_____

_____

The sports I follow are

_____

_____

The ideas that grab my interest are about

_____

_____

The people I care about are involved in

_____

_____

When my spirits or energy are low, then I take time to

_____

_____

The things I'd most like to learn more about are

_____

_____

My good points are

_____

_____

My shortcomings are

_____

_____

The particular activities I like doing the most are

_____

_____

What my family thinks I'm doing with my life up to now

_____

_____

Others I'm around most frequently would likely say they believe I'm all about. . .

How people I do things for would probably describe me and my work

The things I'd most like to learn more about are

For my next birthday, I'd like my friends to

Which of the following are the best and next best short descriptions of you at your finest?

- ❏ Clearly Visionary
- ❏ Effective Leader
- ❏ Extremely Loyal
- ❏ Great Producer
- ❏ Highly Dependable
- ❏ Insightful Advisor
- ❏ Solidly Spiritual
- ❏ Very Well Liked
- ❏ Widely Trusted

My other good qualities

_____

_____

_____

If income and responsibilities were not a consideration, I'd like to . . .
(describe what activities you would engage in just to satisfy yourself)

_____

_____

_____

_____

_____

_____

If I could do whatever I wanted for a day, I would . . .

_____

_____

_____

If I could do whatever I wanted for a month, I would . . .

_____

_____

_____

If I could do whatever I wanted for two years, I would . . .

_____

_____

_____

The story, fable, myth fairy tale, or other anecdote which seems most relevant to my life experience is . . .

(Please relate the parts that are most significant to you.)

_____

_____

_____

_____

_____

_____

_____

_____

_____

_____

If I could, I'd like to be known for my . . .

_____

_____

_____

_____

Going forward from now, the best I can imagine or predict, my career might be something like . . .

(Write the position, kind of organizations, type of assignment, how long you'd expect to spend with each, how changes and transitions might come about, what important things you would do besides work, what you would do when you are successful enough not to have to work.)

NOW
_____

_____

_____

_____

_____

_____

NEXT
_____

_____

_____

_____

_____

_____

AFTER THAT
_____

_____

_____

_____

FURTHER

ETCETERA

Chapter Eight
Finding Your First Job

The difficulty in life is the choice.
—George Moore

*Everyone has been made for some particular work, and the
desire for that work has been put in every heart.*
—Rumi

If you're graduating soon, think of this transition period as something like your old growing pains—a temporary discomfort to endure for the sake of fervently wished-for results. No matter how sophisticated your academic program has been, you'll need to make way for a tremendous adjustment. Making the transition from school to your first post-school full-time job is a tremendous undertaking. You can plunge in recklessly as so many others have done, or you can make some intelligent preparations. Your career center has programs and services which can help, so you don't have to do this alone.

Besides providing a good basis for starting a relationship with your counselor, career center workshops offer practical information you'll absolutely need. One of the most popular is the résumé-writing workshop, in which you see a variety of types, pick the best one for you, and then actually draft a copy.

Q. How do I find out what jobs are available?

A. Here are seven ways of finding out about job sources:
1. Log onto JOBTRAK, available 24 hours a day online at most universities.
2. Call the automated telephone Jobline listings.
3. Visit the career library; there's a room full of information that you can read about employers.
4. Talk to a career counselor.

5. Click onto your career center's and other colleges' Internet pages.
6. Ask your professors for leads.
7. Scour the bulletin boards in your major's department office.

What You Really Need to Know About Résumés

Most employers want a résumé, a one-page summary that fairly represents your education, work experience, and relevant activities to entice an employer's interest in interviewing you. This short précis, neither overly modest nor boastful, is harder to write than it seems. Most students welcome assistance by a trained counselor even when they have access to online job-search services that allow job-seekers to enter information about themselves directly into a database. Résumés are still a necessity. Your résumé must look professional. That means clean, printed on white paper with even margins, proofread by someone reliable so that it's perfect.

But all good counselors and all successfully employed people will tell you that even though you need to have a résumé, it will not get you the job. A résumé is only a tool to get you an interview. Even though writing a résumé is a difficult process, it serves as proof—even better than a business card—that you exist, and are accurately describing your education and experiences. Writing your résumé does help you become explicit about what you have done

But avoid the trap that most people fall into: Crafting a résumé, mailing out hundreds of copies, then sitting back lulled into believing that the job hunting is done. Not true. Not even close. In fact, in most cases you won't even be called. Few potential employers respond to résumés because these pieces of paper are passive, noninteractive, and can easily be filed away to be taken care of "later." And even if employers do respond, you must remember that your résumé is competing with hundreds of others.

Here's what you have to do if you're graduating. Certainly compose your résumé, both on paper and on online résumé matching services. JOBTRAK, a job listing service available at most college's career centers, also has a résumé service. All you need is a password on your center's computer for the menu to enter your data concerning education and experience.

Career Qs

Q: How do I write my résumé?

A. The most typical version is just a direct account of yourself, telling where to contact you and why you're qualified. You list your education and experience backwards, going from the present to the past.
1. Heading: name, address, phone (plus fax/E-mail). (Include your parent's address as your permanent one if you live off or near campus)
2. Education at college, listing majors, activities, and honors (don't list high school)
3. Work (part and full time) with titles, dates, responsibilities
4. Volunteer activities
5. Skills: e.g., computer or language
6. References: state that they are available (List your references on a separate page and have letters of recommendation ready.)

Do not list: Height, weight, expected salary, hobbies, marriages, or obligations, or even your GPA unless you're in the top 15 percent. The point is to get an interview, not to raise issues to disqualify yourself.

Career Qs

Q: What is a cover letter?

A cover letter accompanies your résumé to explain why you are applying for a position in straightforward language. You end by asking for and interview, which you'll call to schedule.

The Story of JOBTRAK

You'll probably use JOBTRAK, the electronic job listing service, in your job search. How JOBTRAK was created is an interesting story in itself.

> JOBTRAK itself was created serendipitously by Connie and Ken
> Ramberg. As a graduating senior from Stanford University, Ken
> was bent on finding a job in investment banking. Ken had pre-

viously studied in Italy and worked in the marketing department for DHL in Hong Kong. He hoped that this background would jump-start his career in international finance. It was while searching through hundreds of job listings posted on the career center's bulletin boards that Ken recognized the need for computerizing this information, and began formulating a plan for a totally different career.

At the same time, his entrepreneurial mother, Connie, had been approached by a friend with a business plan to create a national database of employer profiles for college students. Having worked as a management consultant, Connie had guided clients to college career centers to find qualified employees. Calling career centers one by one, however, was a tedious process, and it was at this point she recognized the need for a one-stop call center which would allow employers to post job listings on college campuses nationwide.

Meanwhile, Ken was intent on landing a job in the world of high finance. The eighties were the high-flying years in investment banking and the competition for jobs was fierce. After two months of networking, phone calls, sending résumés and going on interviews, he was hired into the corporate finance division at Bear Stearns & Co.

While Connie and partner David Franey worked on the JOB-TRAK business during the days, Ken came to the office in the evenings to assist. All three partners recognized the vast opportunities created by the inefficient, cumbersome way employers posted jobs on campus and students, in turn, searched through the listings. Solving those two problems launched a new, more efficient service for career centers, students, employers and themselves—a win-win-win-win service. Today, over 600 colleges participate in the JOBTRAK service and more than 300,000 employers have posted job opportunities on the network. In 1992, JOBTRAK received the Entrepreneur of the Year award by the governor of California.

Career Qs

Q. I'm an accounting major with some prior sales experience and need to find a job soon. I've looked through JobTrak but don't think I have a chance with the Big Six. Any suggestions?

A. Here's how to work an electronic job listing service like JOBTRAK: Don't get lost in predetermined categories. Broaden your fishing net. As it turns out, the Big Six accounting and management consulting firms aren't hiring so many new accountants, preferring more experienced CPA's who don't need expensive training programs. Therefore, when you're job hunting, think small- to mid-sized firms. Get a list of these companies from the career center or your accounting department. Submit your résumé for recruiting to both sources.

Plus, think of what you like or sold in the past, and search for positions in accounting departments in companies you are familiar with already. Open your net to catch every area: cars, athletic equipment, food, computers, film, even the IRS. Focus on companies and industries as well. Use the online service and get more information by clicking onto those organizations. Go after such appropriate positions—even if they're not listed. Think of JOBTRAK as more of an idea source, not just a bank from which you withdraw a selected job. In addition, find out when your college's next Job Fair or campus recruiting days are. Bring a dozen copies of your résumé and a friendly manner to land yourself a job offer.

References

Prospective employers are likely to ask you for references. Make a list of your best professors, coaches, club sponsors, employers, and family friends, and file it at your career center or on your own computer job search file—which you'll keep adding to forever. Be sure to include addresses for each of your references. Be strategic about which people you ask for letters of recommendation to include in that file and help them out by drafting the letters that you'd wish they would write, including an example of work, activities, leadership, and contributions or inventions. Try for a range of references—a professor in your major area, a supervisor, a faculty administrator, a former employer, and prominent family friend, if you know one.

Follow through! After you've send your résumés and cover letters, you have to telephone to schedule an interview. Often you'll have to call every day for two weeks. But your goal is to get an interview as the key to getting a job offer.

JOB FAIRS

College career centers regularly conduct job fairs inviting employers to explain their companies on campus and to recruit students for positions, even internships. At a job fair, you'll have a chance to talk to hundreds of employers to find out what they do, what they're looking for, where there's some opportunity for you. And there will be, but only if you take the initiative to give out your résumé and get information. You have to take a risk, be curious, friendly, and ask questions of them. At the same time, you have to ask them to schedule an interview. No one will discover you, alas. So it all depends on your making something happen.

At a job fair, as in real life, you get a minute to present as good an image of yourself as possible. Remember, a firm handshake, a clear, audible voice, and a ready smile. Take their business cards if you're interested and make notes to yourself on the reverse side. Ask employers you're interested in what steps to take to follow up.

Career Qs

Q. Do I need to bring a résumé to the Job Fair? A cover letter?

A. Yes to the résumé. Bring twelve copies just in case. Offer copies to the employers you talk to and find interesting. Your conversation is your cover letter. Make sure it serves the purposes a cover letter would. So make yourself talk about your skills, major, best courses, and interests. Ask for their advice, experience—and a job offer.

Career Qs

Q. What do I wear to the Job Fair?

A. Graduating seniors, leave your jeans at home, and wear appropriate business attire (e.g., a jacket and tie, or skirt). Bring a folder for your résumés and a pad of paper as well as an envelope for collecting business cards. Be sure to look as prepared and professional as you will to your interviews. You won't make a mistake in dressing more like the interviewer than like your classmate.

Career Qs

Q. How do I follow up after a Job Fair?

A. If you asked those employers whom you were interested in for best ways to contact them, follow their advice. Do not wait for them to discover or remember to call you. Send them a letter. Always write how glad you were to meet them, include your résumé (again), and ask for an appointment. Then call them. Be sure to get their names spelled right and learn how to pronounce them. Then you must keep the appointments you make. Dress the way managers do at their businesses. Arrive early with another copy of your résumé (again), and a list of your references plus your letters of recommendation.

To prepare yourself, make an appointment to see your career counselor and sign up for a workshop on interviewing.

Find out all you can about the organization—what it does, who it hires, what it pays, along with its advancement practices and culture. You can find all this out; it takes a search that the career center can help you with.

INTERVIEW STRATEGIES

Most college career centers offer practice in interviewing. Sign up for a workshop (or private session) so you can learn how to present yourself well enough to land a job. Mock interviews and videotape sessions, though difficult, even agonizing to go through at the time, allow you to see and improve on how you appear to interviewers. It will be the fastest learning experience you can undertake—and an immediately rewarding one.

Sign up for every employer interview for which you qualify, no matter whether you are vitally interested in the company or not. Consider it practice so that you can understand what an employer wants to accomplish in the interview. Essentially, their goal is not so much finding the smartest person for the job, but rather it is finding the right person for the right job. You'll learn how to be that right person if you want the job.

What Interviewers Really Want to Find Out

Don't play the "good student." Employers don't want students. They want enthusiastic, contributing employees. They want employees who have excellent written, computer, and oral skills as well as collaboration skills. To determine how you stack up as a potential employee, they ask you questions to tell them whether you've had any experience, what your past studies have been like, where you see yourself in five years, what strengths and weaknesses you have. I have even heard one interviewer ask, "If you were a leaf on a tree, where would you place yourself?"

These are all strategic questions designed to get you to answer the implicit, although illegal, question that holds the key to what they really what want to know: Are you enough like them to make them want to make you a member of their team? They want you to be similar to them—similar in values, intent, background, and vision. That translates to work ethic, politics, even humor. You have to explain who you are by carefully selecting your experiences in school activities, part-time jobs, relevant interests, and internships and showing how each project or involvement demonstrates your skills and accomplishments.

Does this sound very manipulative to you? Then consider how you pick friends. You want them to like you and *be* like you. You want friend to value, even mirror, your ideas and feelings. The more you share ideas and feelings, no matter how different you may appear on the surface, the closer you become. There is a saying that we think smart people are those who think we are smart. That's pretty true. If you disagree, then think of whom you have asked for advice about which professor to study with or which course to take, even what movies to see. I'd be willing to bet that you ask only those whose tastes and judgments turn out to be the same as yours. Why? You want someone who will validate and support your own instincts about what to do. This isn't idiosyncratic behavior. It's human nature. We all do it.

Career Qs

Q: What can I expect from job interviews?

A. Here's a quick overview of interviewing, '90s style.

- *Expect long interviews—two hours plus—and multiple interviewers who might meet with you all at once, or sometimes in a series of one-on-ones. Practice self-defense. Ask how long an interview will last and how many people you will meet. Try to get a breather between meetings to refresh yourself and review how you've done.*

- *Instead of standard, predictable questions like, "What is your greatest strength?" you will be asked for particular behaviors or skills, for example, "Tell me about a time when you worked under tremendous stress."*

- *Rehearse effective ways of describing important accomplishment to interviewers. Have at least three examples of skills you want to highlight, so you won't repeat yourself.*

- *It's okay to bring and refer to documents that corroborate your achievements—charts, publications, reports, and so on.*

- *You need to know that meals are not purely social occasions. Never let down your guard.*

Be Prepared to Participate

In addition to demonstrating similar values, you have to continue to actively participate in the interview itself. It is not a one-way test, but rather more like a dialogue. You, too, have to come prepared with questions to ask about the company and even about the interviewers themselves. You might ask about an interviewer's experience and background, his lapel pin or the corporate logo, how they celebrate success on the job at his company, whether and how the company promotes from within.

If you have trouble with this casual way of talking, pretend you are a newspaper reporter. Show interest by following up with questions after their statements. Ask questions such as How did your company grow so fast in the last year? Why did the company adopt that policy? When did you become a recruiter? Who were your mentors? And at the end of the interview thank the interviewer for his time; say you enjoyed meeting him. And if you want the job, ask for it then and there.

Ask if the company can hire you immediately. If they say that they're still in the process of considering other candidates, ask if they have any concerns about you so that you can explain or defend yourself. That way, you still have a chance to make a stronger pitch. For example, if they say that they'd prefer someone with more experience, then you quickly scan over your past and cite activities that you've participated in, offices you ran for, and projects you undertook in your classes. For example, here are some reasonable responses: "You're right; I haven't taken any accounting course. But I served as class treasurer and was responsible for managing a budget of . . . ." "While I haven't worked for a computer company, I'm the unofficial techie in my group, always able to solve a difficult problem, and usually working on the latest software. I'm certain I can perform for you."

Your enthusiastic defense of yourself will often suffice. Remember: It is always better to present yourself assertively than to secretly hope they will discover the real, talented, wonderful you. And after all, you are just beginning your career life. You can expect that you'll learn fast and grow professionally. If you feel some tension at this stage of the interview, you might also ask how the interviewer how he got his start, and who gave him his break.

Take the Ball and Run

> *Job interviewer: "So, what kind of student are you?"*
> *Student job seeker: "Um . . . okay?"*

Here's an example of a dumb question and an even dumber answer that I actually overheard at a job fair. The rule? No matter what the quality of question interviewers ask, you have to be savvy enough to take the ball and run with it. In response to the question, "What kind of student are you?" you have to do better than a one-word answer. If you want the job, "okay" is not okay. You have to continue with "I'm a fine student and I especially enjoy the research aspect. Here's how I presented my findings . . ." or, "I enjoy my science labs the most because I'm self-directed . . ." or "My best work comes in collaboration with others; for example . . . ." The key? You mention your best course or subject and then illustrate how or why with a backup reason or example. No matter their questions, you are the one who manipulates the answers. You select your own traits, skills, and behaviors that show you off as the best choice for an employee.

You can't count on improvisational skills when you're on the spot unless you're an experienced actor. So rather than winging it and hoping for the best, make yourself prepare with the help of your career counselor:

1. Reread your own résumé.

2. Explain why and how you excelled in your best classes and papers and projects.

3. Explain the importance to you of your activities and the roles you played.

4. Think of a few career choices you'd like and why you'd expect to do well.

Learn the art of weaving examples of your experiences and skills into an interesting response. And, even though it's serious, smile. Friendliness counts as much as neatness. No one wants to hire a grump. And be lively. Ask about your interviewer's experience and past. Remember, an interview is more like a dance than a test with only right answers. Say you're really interested in the job, if you are.

Far from sounding conceited, you'll sound confident. Remember to ask when you can expect to hear from them. And, send a handwritten thank-you note. You can find samples in the career center.

Career Qs

Q. I'm scheduled for a job interview I'd like to get, but I'm not positive I qualify. How can I be sure?

A. You're really asking two questions: how to ace an interview and how to qualify yourself. Interviewing is an amazing art. You've got to show you're skilled, enthusiastic, and a fine team player. For tips on what that looks like, come view the videotapes in the career center's library and take a workshop. You'll see what immediately qualifies and disqualifies you. For example, interviews are not tests: There are no absolute right answers. So, even if you don't have the exact experience the prospective employer wants, you can answer questions without lying and still get the job. "Have you done this before?" can be answered, "I have had related experience in working on a volunteer project, taking direction and handling budgets" (or plans, program, clients, etcetera). Or, "I have worked on a business project with my team and designed (or made or researched, and so on.) Never answer with only a few words. Don't wait for the next question. Ask the interviewers about their own experiences. Ask for the job. Don't disqualify yourself by assuming they won't want you, or they won't.

It's hard; everyone's blown an interview. I cried once during an interview, and later, in my car, pounded the steering wheel vowing it would never happen again. It didn't.

Job hunting can be a treacherous process, but it is requisite to getting hired. You have to offer yourself enthusiastically and positively to people you don't even know for jobs you aren't sure of—all with no guarantees you'll get the offer. Most times you won't; it's all depending on numbers, timing, luck, as well as your interviewing skills, background, and demonstration you can do the job even if you've never done it before. How many interviews do you go after? As many as it takes to get a good job. If they show some interest in you, but aren't sure that you're experienced enough, offer to work for the company on a trial basis (for a week to a month) to prove yourself to them.

Career Qs

Q. I just mailed my résumé out to many companies and I faxed some. Which is the right way? I hear I need a cover letter. Does that mean I've ruined my chances?

A. What's the "right" way to send a résumé? Whatever gets you the job offer. If the company requests either a mailed or faxed copy of your résumé, comply. But if you're sending it on your own, mail it. No matter how you get it there, you must include a cover letter to explain which job you're applying for and why your experience is relevant. Attend a quick résumé writing seminar at your career center.

But you can't just send résumés out and sit back, waiting for responses. You have to take charge of the next step: calling for appointments and learning how to interview.

NEGOTIATING YOUR FIRST JOB OFFER: DOS AND DON'TS

- When you do get a job offer, try to get as much information about what the job really entails and then ask for a salary range; choose high, trying to get as much as you can get in salary and benefits.

- Don't take what's first offered just because you're so grateful. Don't worry, you'll more than earn your salary. Try to get an appropriate salary first even if you have to bite the bullet and negotiate for it. The best way to negotiate a good salary is to make your prospective employer state the range first; don't be the first to throw out a number. Then you can counter with fifty percent more than what you want. The usual compromise is somewhere in between, so you have to aim high.

- The truth is that most people don't start out making much money. It helps to check into the average amount or at least know the range; you'll get such information at the career center. You'll be a better negotiator if you know the going rates. Even though you would like more and need it to repay loans or to buy a new car, you still have to have some patience.

- Don't think that you should accept anything to get in hoping that once you're there and they recognize your talents, they will raise you to what you're really worth.

- You don't have to respond immediately to an offer. You can always say, "Let me think about this and see what is best." Then run like mad to check with your counselor and friends. It doesn't always work, but it's worth trying.

- Make sure you've talked to the person you'll work for. If there's bad chemistry, ask for another interview to get a second impression. You don't have to love your boss, but it helps if you respect him or her.

- Sometimes you will suffer from the best kind of problem: two competing offers to choose from. If one employer offers more opportunity to learn and grow but less money to start, you might risk it after checking with others who've been there before you. Or if an employer is in a new field or one that is so compelling to you, then take a chance. Most often people choose the larger, more comprehensive company that has name recognition and a respected training program.

- Write a thank-you note to show your appreciation, reiterate your interest in the job, as well as a few of your strongest assets that make you the best candidate.

To start, prepare and rehearse a minute's self-presentation. It's hard to do; getting coached or taped will improve your delivery. Most of us hate this part, feeling artificial, fraudulent, pushy. You'll become your walking, talking résumé: (re)introducing yourself in an interesting, positive, friendly but pointed way. You tell the facts about yourself, what you have to offer, and then ask for their contacts or help in giving your written résumé to the right people. Then you follow up with a written note with your thanks, and a call to report (*not* complain about) your progress or lack of it, and suggestions for next steps. Follow up and repeat the process.

You'll keep a file of business leads so you can remember to cite their names, business cards with notes about these people on the reverse sides to jog your memory, letters you write and receive, and promises to keep.

Together with these contacts you meet, you're on the way to discover the true heart in our work life. It will be your turn soon.

Career Qs

Q: I hear that networking is the real way to find a job. How do I start?

A. Your goal is to find people who will be helpful to you in your job search by providing other contacts, information, and advice. They will be professors, counselors, administrators, staff, employers, club sponsors, alumni, family and family friends. You have to invite their participation in your search by revealing who you are (your talents, skills, accomplishments), your dreams (ultimate career) or specific goal (a job now), why you're asking them (they're smart and connected), and what help you'd like from them (from a job to job leads).

Strategies for the Job Search

Practice job interviews.

Be brave. Get videotaped while you rehearse job interviewing. Take a look at yourself; retake the video and see how you improve. Get coaching. Learn to describe what you've learned in classes and clubs, internships and work. Tell why you'd make a great employee. Don't pretend you know a lot; you're not supposed to. Ask for the job. Ask what concerns an employer has about you and try to answer them. If you can't counter an employer's reservations about you, just say you're willing to learn.

Get up and go after jobs.

Don't wait for recruiters to arrive on campus. Find people written about in the newspaper or interviewed on T.V. See if you can establish some link; ask for even a temporary job.

Hustle.

Not just a '70s dance craze or an illegal occupation. Hustling—going after what you think you might want (even if you don't really have a clue)—means connecting your interests and abilities to the marketplace and seeing where convergence happens. You'll learn to act for yourself, not just fulfill assignments.

Don't wait for a prestigious name to launch you.

Don't depend on the prestige of your college or university to launch you into the world. Combine hustle with theory. It'll be more fun than you think. And it's the juice of the real world, no matter whether it's a place in academia, science, entertainment, or sales that you're after.

Chapter Nine
Making the Transition

We know what we are, not what we may become.
—William Shakespeare

There is no future in any job. The future lies in the one
who holds the job.
—Street wisdom

Making the great transition from student to employee takes concerted effort. It doesn't just come naturally. Woody Allen once quipped that the most important skill is "just showing up." There's a lot to that; showing up requires self-discipline and the willingness to belong. If you've been used to a fairly independent or downright flaky schedule, this will be harder than you'd imagine. So do show up, on time, well groomed, and with an enthusiastic attitude. You'll have to give up your expectations that your job will be explicitly laid out for you, that you'll be regularly graded or appreciated, and receive raises and promotions every six months or at least every year. You'll have to learn how to ask for feedback during and at the end of projects so that you can deliver what's expected and improve your skills. "How am I doing? Is there any other way to accomplish this that I should try?" are good questions to ask your supervisor to get started. And when you get criticism, don't blow it by being defensive. Listen, repeat what you heard, and reply somewhat respectfully, "Point taken," or "Show me how you'd like me to improve." Later, check back with your supervisor to see if you're on target. Show your appreciation for the feedback. This is the first step towards being coached well.

Some rules to start:

1. Despite what you think, your basic job is to make your boss look good. You must always do that.

2. Don't complain about the job or backstab the people you work for: You'll be labeled a loser.

3. Don't ask your boss to solve your problems without thinking out a plan for the solutions yourself.

4. Learn to compliment those people whom you see doing well, including your bosses, no matter what their rank is.

5. Learn who's there and who's who and who does what. Ask people about their work, their projects, their lives.

Career Qs

Q. I'm in my senior year in computer science. I already have several job offers that pay so much that I'd be out of debt and could even replace my car. I'm thinking of taking the best-paying job now full time and finishing college later. What do you think?

A. I think not, even though these offers are tempting. My advice is to work part time and take advantage of internships to have a better view of the many opportunities that you really do have. But finish your bachelor's degree now for a solid foundation. Don't worry that these job offers will evaporate. They will, in fact, only increase. As technology becomes increasingly complex, the best opportunities will go to those with college degrees, proving that you are able to learn how to learn. Your diploma will therefore become even more valuable. If you need a breather and some padding for your bank account, put off graduate school for a few years, but don't interrupt your undergraduate education. Ask your department chair and professors, I think they would agree with me.

Don't be afraid the first job won't last. It probably won't last. Everything changes. The jobs will. The marketplace will. And best of all, you will. You're starting the first part of your first career. There's no set map to find your way to the next part. Advancement or change comes only through following on a hunch or from a great project or following a great boss who is promoted and takes you along. Or you find a position that's newly created. Or you decide to go to graduate school and follow a different track. Or you discover an aspect of a project, another project, or a whole new area that absorbs you totally.

Career Qs

Q. I am pursuing a B.S. in biology but find that class, work, and family is very demanding. I just heard that I need a master's degree to succeed in science. Is this true?

A. Yes, it is. We're empathetic about the number of sacrifices it requires to juggle classes, studying, work, family, even friends at this time in your life. But if you are in a technical field (e.g., life sciences), you do need an advanced degree for long-term, highly technical career opportunities. The very same holds for professional degrees such as medicine, dentistry, or pharmacy. However, if you can't go on to graduate school right now, or you don't want to do highly technical work, look for other rewarding science-related work that doesn't require a master's degree. You may be surprised to learn that many biology majors find interesting and lucrative opportunities in sales—for example, pharmaceutical, or medical products—as well as in business. Teaching, a field requiring a credential which you can get from night school, is another possibility. There are many science positions available right now.

You have a variety of choices; a session with your career counselor can help prioritize them and get you started in the interviewing process.

College commencement is literally our moving on—on to the world of work, on to a full-time career. *Career* is a more accurate word than *work*. *Career* implies a great constellation, more significant than simply performing one task for pay so that we can live. For most of us, our work is our identity. We experience life through our chosen frameworks. Scientists view the world differently from the way artists or corporate managers do. What we do becomes who we are. You have been living these past years as a student, thinking of yourself as a "student." Finally the time comes to make an enormous leap, a transition to a new identity.

But we resist most change because moving to a new or an unknown set of circumstances is uncomfortable, even anxiety provoking. Seeing ourselves in new situations often leads to identity crises that are difficult to live through. However much you think you can prepare, you can't direct or stop your emotions. Everyone who changes goes through a psychological shift. The awkwardness of transitioning from college can be shorter-lived if you began to develop the life skills you'll need to develop while you were still in college. For, the more you experience and risk, the more open you are to opportunity, the more you will accomplish.

THE ROAD AHEAD: TOP TEN CAREER STRATEGIES FOR GRADS

Once you've gotten your job and started on your career, now's the time to read *Skills for Success* and *Career Strategies for the Working Woman*. (The latter book is not limited to women only; there's information everyone can use.) In the meantime, here are ten quick strategies for career success.

1. Develop yourself into an expert. Are you great at digging out hidden facts? Do you have a natural gift for socializing? Build on these strengths no matter what your job description is and you'll find people turning to you. And you'll create the job you're best suited to.

2. Study those whom the leaders in your company and your field rely on. Read biographies of great achievers, paying attention to how they learned to recognize opportunities. Learn from them. Make them your mentors by trying out their advice.

3. Join a professional association and do more than just attend monthly meetings. Volunteer for a committee. Find out whose working style you admire and work with that person. Experiment with your own transactional style and/or subject interests. Take time to meet not only the invited speakers but those at your table. *Use* them in the best sense of the word: Ask their opinions and advice; report back and thank them. Practice your leadership skills here where you can't be fired.

4. Make yourself visible on the job. Build relationships not just with your peers but your bosses too. Write memos that demonstrate your knowledge and your work. Volunteer for task forces or special committees. Speak up at meetings in a positive way.

5. Start small. Initiate informal conversation with your boss, even your boss's boss whom you meet casually (in the elevator, or parking lot); ask a question, and make comments. At the next question-answer period of a conference, stand up, introduce yourself, compliment the speaker, then ask a question or make a comment. Become a player, a real member of the team.

6. Make your bosses look good. Provide your bosses with what they need to thrive—new markets or products and researched ideas. Find out what they need to be successful: learn to contribute all you can. Let your ideas flow. You won't be disappointed.

7. If you want to take action but you feel nervous, imagine that you are the most successful and courageous person you admire and do what he or she would do. Or do what most of us do: Simulate or practice feeling confident, and self-confidence will become yours. Faking courage leads to action which, in turn, builds courage.

8. Do the work assigned to you as well as you can. Get feedback and learn to improve.

9. Once you've worked for your company for a while, look around inside for leads to richer opportunities, more interesting projects, and higher-ranking and better-paying jobs. Meet with those who have these jobs and find out more about what they do, and if it interests you, ask what you have to do to work for them. Or, after a few years, jump over the fence and work for the other side if you're dissatisfied. For example, switch from being a private C.P.A. to IRS specialist or vice-versa. In this leap, you'll use some of the same skills you've already acquired, but you'll have a new environment to explore.

10. Make lifelong learning your personal motto. If you're alive, you're not done learning. Ask your professors for advice. Send for graduate school catalogs. Apply to a variety of programs. Ask about fellowships, grants, and specialized programs. Consider night or weekend programs for pursuing your graduate studies. Don't limit yourself to daytime programs.

My life's work has been devoted to discovering how and why people do what they do. I have found that each of us is inspired, nourished, encouraged, and confirmed by the loving support from others. We are, in addition, emboldened and transformed through our will to risk, to try, to take a chance. Everything is open to you—if you are willing to go for it.

Chapter Ten
Strategy Checklists

A journey of 1,000 miles begins with one step.
—Chinese Proverb

Throughout this book, I have suggested behaviors and attitudes to put into play in undergraduate and graduate school. Use the following summary to stimulate you to action, to spur you on when you fall into the passive-student trap, so that you can make opportunities for yourself.

Remember that success starts with small steps—learning to try, experimenting, and expanding. Only in this process does the essence of success—courage, care, and mission—have a chance to flourish. Happy adventures in your careering!

WHAT TO DO WHEN: A SCHEDULE TO ACHIEVE YOUR GOALS AND BEAT THE "GOOD" STUDENT TRAP

Freshman Year: Getting Oriented

○ Succeed in your courses. Get to know your professors and ask how you can improve.

○ Form a study group with three or four other students and use the group well.

○ Apply for work-study through the financial aid office, or for a part-time job through your career center during the academic year and over the summer.

- ○ Join one club or activity and become active.

- ○ Join in one day-long volunteer activity.

Sophomore Year: Playing the Field

- ○ Declare your major. Start taking interesting electives, no matter how unrelated they seem.

- ○ Join another club; step up your involvement.

- ○ Connect your assigned papers to your interests.

- ○ Talk to your professors and begin asking their advice.

- ○ Sign up for an internship for the summer.

- ○ Investigate your chances for your junior year abroad or in another state.

Junior Year: Getting Serious

- ○ Take at least one internship in a field you're curious about.

- ○ Ask your professors for help in connecting your papers to your major.

- ○ Ask one professor to let you rewrite a paper with guidance to learn the process of writing . . . even without credit.

- ○ Run for office for your club; get involved in its national organization.

- ○ Find another interesting club to join just for new ideas.

- ○ Sign up for a class offering Service Learning.

○ Get involved in a volunteer activity.

○ Visit the career center for assessments, private sessions, workshops, and internship and job leads.

○ If necessary, change your major or add another one.

Senior Year: Pulling it All Together

○ Make your assigned papers catapult you inside organizations. Try to present or publish one of them.

○ Take a résumé-writing workshop and write a few résumés with a couple of cover letters.

○ Attend job fairs and career conferences with dozens of résumés in hand.

○ Learn interviewing techniques through workshops and try them out.

○ Get letters of recommendation (after writing the first drafts yourself) from professors, employers, counselors, and others now while they remember you.

○ Network with employers during career events, alumni in your field, and people whom your professors recommend. Follow up with calls to schedule appointments.

○ Use the clubs you've joined to invite prospective employers to speak.

○ Get an internship in the very organization you want to work for and make that happen.

○ Investigate graduate school; decide whether to apply now or later.

○ Make time to do a real job search; don't panic and settle.

○ Ask for coaching for interviewing and negotiating.

○ Sign up for the alumni association to support your college.

Note: Most colleges extend reciprocity for services like those offered in a career center. If your college doesn't have one, or if you move, you can usually come to another college's career center, sometimes for a small fee. And if you still can't find the direction you want, make an appointment with a professional career counselor or career strategist. Don't think that the answers will just come into your head; as with everything else, you have to go find them and make them work.

GETTING THE MOST OUT OF YOUR CLASSES, WORK, ACTIVITIES, AND CAREER COUNSELING SERVICES

Professors and Classroom Behavior

(Freshman and Sophomores)

○ Ask questions in class.

○ Get involved in class discussions.

○ Form private study groups, meet regularly, don't cram.

○ Find and read professors' work.

○ Find out which professors are most respected through recommendations, ratings, even by reading *Who's Who*, and book indices.

○ Visit professors during office hours to build a relationship so that you can investigate subjects that interest you and find mentors and advocates for your studies.

(Juniors and Seniors)

○ Find out what research or special projects are going on in your department and join in on any basis, from volunteer to paid professional.

Other Professional Relationships

○ Get to know your advisors and staff to find out information about special programs, financial aid, grants, internships, and work-study opportunities. Introduce yourself, ask questions, and read bulletin boards and participate in events.

○ Ask about independent study, exchanging one class for another, increasing your load, or taking an advanced class.

○ Meet the dean of your school formally by attending open meetings and lectures as well as informally by stopping by during office hours.

Assigned Papers and Projects

○ Aim to finish your assignments early so that you can meet with your professor (or teaching assistant) for feedback on the structure and content of the work you've done. Prepare a first draft and schedule a consultation to provide you with a framework of ideas. Although this might sound impossible, you can do it. And taking these extra steps will enhance your performance in college.

○ Seek out people in your chosen field who can be willing to act as your mentors or advisors, providing you with actual case materials from their businesses.

○ Compare your papers with your classmates' work. Learn how to express ideas.

○ Form a study group and learn to discuss intellectual concepts and collaborate on projects.

○ Write your papers with an extra purpose in mind. Try to publish them in a campus newspaper or magazine, or in a professional journal or a popular publication.

○ Think of using your papers and assignments from various classes to explore a particular area from several different angles. Each academic assignment might then build on a concept that could be expanded into a thesis or dissertation.

Essay Tests

○ Approach your professor early with questions when essay topics have been assigned. Show an outline of your answer to determine whether the substance and style are appropriate.

○ Compose each answer as an entire essay with a defined beginning, middle, and end.

○ Learn to think about what the facts mean instead of merely reciting them by rote. Discover what recognized theorists believe and figure out what you think, whether you agree or disagree.

○ Discuss your exams afterward with your professors to find out how you can improve your answering style or where you went wrong or misunderstood. Don't worry about changing your grade; concentrate on learning to think.

○ Take notes during or immediately after these sessions; it's easy to forget what is difficult to hear.

Standardized Tests

○ Find out as much about the test in advance. Learn about the format of the questions, and the content that will be covered.

○ If you intend to apply for graduate or professional school, find out what admission tests are necessary. Get samples of the tests. Be aware of application deadlines. Start studying well in advance of the test, whether you're studying on your own or taking a prep course.

Clubs and Activities

○ Find out the array of activities—debate, orchestra, literary journal—from the student organization office, other students, or professors. Visit the first meeting of several clubs to see which are the most interesting to you. Then join.

○ Find ways to become active. Volunteer for a committee.

○ Build an area of expertise within a club, and commit yourself to deliver what you have promised. You might sample several clubs or specialize in one club or activity and take it to the limits.

○ Experiment with different aspects and roles (supporter, leader, redirector, champion).

○ Develop strong relationships with the sponsor, faculty, and staff surrounding that activity.

○ Find business, arts, and service contacts outside the campus—all of whom might be interested in your club's activity.

Work

○ Find a job that you may want to keep for your college career. Start with perfecting even the most menial tasks. Once you prove your loyalty and competence, you will be able to advance. Don't be shy about using "connections," or asking for help or opportunities.

○ Think of a job as a social experience and take time to meet all kinds of students and employees.

○ Treat each job as if it were your own business. Think of how you would run it, in terms of management, employee motivation, customer relations, accounting, etcetera.

○ Find existing internships or create your own, on or off campus. Find out what other students have done and learned from their experiences.

○ Find opportunities to meet local business or professional people— talk about your experiences and ask about theirs.

○ Work as a teaching assistant to gain experience in lecturing or managing.

○ Work as a research assistant in a laboratory or on a project if you are interested in developing ideas, working with a team, or considering graduate school.

○ Pay as much attention to the way in which you work with people as you do in completing the task itself.

Career Counseling Services

○ Go to your college's career center early to discover what it offers.

○ Establish a friendly relationship with career counselors. When they've helped you, let them know it. Suggest other means of assistance, and volunteer to make arrangements if necessary.

○ Find out what interests you, then explore the field with assistance from your career counselor.

○ If you don't know what you want to do, ask for guidance. Investigate several different fields to see which beckons to you. Find a related internship.

○ Take workshops and seminars to learn what professionals do, as well as to discover or confirm your interests.

○ Start your placement file with letters of recommendation from professors whose courses you have recently taken and excelled in. It may help if you draft a letter for them, although this might be very difficult for you to do at first. Ask a career counselor to show you some sample letters of recommendation. Make copies and keep the originals in a safe place along with diplomas, transcripts, birth certificate, licenses, and your social security card.

❍ Sign up for interviewing sessions. Have your session videotaped. Ask for coaching to improve your presentation.

❍ Use every opportunity to interview with recruiters, even if you are not totally committed to their companies or fields.

❍ Be sure to contact alumni in your field of interest for informational interviews, for advice, and for job leads.

Appendix
Resources

The good news is that there is so much information available to guide you through the process of living and learning. The bad news is that there is so much more than you'll ever be able to find time to take in. And it comes in a variety of media from electronic search engines to the old-fashioned paper stuff. What's included in these information listings is not ever exclusive. Remember the motto "Everything changes?" Well, information does, too. The only skills that remain the same are the most human skills of building courage, developing networking skills, and growing professionally—and they take learning and practicing and perfecting.

There are books synonymous with providing the most useful and current resourceful information. Dick Bolles, of *What Color Is Your Parachute?* fame, has dedicated himself to listing resources and provides one of the best. Search through his annually updated lists of people, books, catalogs, computer software, audio- and videotapes, courses and seminar training—on the Internet, in printed directories, and newsletters. The easiest way to get started is with the latest edition of his annually updated career resource, *What Color Is Your Parachute?*

The Career Center at Cal State Northridge, like most college career centers, has its own Web page with an ever-changing table of contents. Typical offerings of The Career Center site:

- Resources are listed by area or discipline, for example, Agriculture, Bioscience, Engineering, or Travel.
- Employment resources listed by city, state, or country.
- Resources for various special groups: women, minorities, disabled, returning or retired students. The pages include lists for best employers for people in these groups.

- Helpful information on important career development processes, from working your way through college, to assessing your interests, to finding an internship, to choosing a career, to job hunting. There are books and software with résumé and cover letter samples. Another area is dedicated to career strategies to solve the inevitable dilemmas you're bound to encounter on your first job or your second career, or your third degree.

By all means, surf career center Internet sites. Skimming through directories of occupational titles or newly invented careers could whet your appetite, even create new appetites. Click on http://www.csun.edu/~hfcar009/books.htm#c to access the Cal State Northridge Career Center page. Check out your own school's and other universities' resources, too. To link to universities around the world, as well as to access more great career and educational links, visit the Kaplan Web site at http://www.kaplan.com.

Don't forget about books. Always read the resource lists at the back of books that you find valuable. My own picks of the moment:

Zen and the Art of Making a Living. Laurence G. Boldt. Penguin, 1993.

The 1997 What Color is Your Parachute? Richard Nelson Bolles. Ten Speed Press, 1996.

Majoring in the Rest of Your Life. Carol Carter. Noonday, 1995.

The College Woman's Handbook. Rachel Dobkin and Shana Sippy. Workman, 1995.

Making a Living While Making a Difference. Melissa Everett. Bantam Doubleday Dell, 1995

You don't have to go it alone. There's always a connection to a person, a resource, an idea, a program. Go for it.

For bulk sales to schools, colleges, and universities,
please contact:

Renee Nemire
Simon & Schuster Special Markets
1633 Broadway, 8th Floor
New York, NY 10019

come to us for the best prep

about KAPLAN

"How can you help me?"

From childhood to adulthood, there are points in life when you need to reach an important goal. Whether you want an academic edge, a high score on a critical test, admission to a competitive college, funding for school, or career success, Kaplan is the best source to help get you there. One of the nation's premier educational companies, Kaplan has already helped millions of students get ahead through our legendary courses and expanding catalog of products and services.

"I have to ace this test!"

The world leader in test preparation, Kaplan will help you get a higher score on standardized tests such as the SSAT and ISEE for secondary school, PSAT, SAT, and ACT for college, the LSAT, MCAT, GMAT, and GRE for graduate school, professional licensing exams for medicine, nursing, dentistry, and accounting, and specialized exams for international students and professionals.

Kaplan's courses are recognized worldwide for their high-quality instruction, state-of-the-art study tools and up-to-date, comprehensive information. Kaplan enrolls more than 150,000 students annually in its live courses at 1,200 locations worldwide.

"How can I pay my way?"

As the price of higher education continues to skyrocket, it's vital to get your share of financial aid and figure out how you're going to pay for school. Kaplan's financial aid resources simplify the often bewildering application process and show you how you can afford to attend the college or graduate school of your choice.

KapLoan, The Kaplan Student Loan Information Program,* helps students get key information and advice about educational loans for college and graduate school. Through an affiliation with one of the nation's largest student loan providers, you can access valuable information and guidance on federally insured parent and student loans. Kaplan directs you to the financing you need to reach your educational goals.

"Can you help me find a good school?"

Through its admissions consulting program, Kaplan offers expert advice on selecting a college, graduate school, or professional school. We can also show you how to maximize your chances of acceptance at the school of your choice.

"But then I have to get a great job!"

Whether you're a student or a grad, we can help you find a job that matches your interests. Kaplan can assist you by providing helpful assessment tests, job and employment data, recruiting services, and expert advice on how to land the right job. Crimson & Brown Associates, a division of Kaplan, is the leading collegiate diversity recruiting firm helping top-tier companies attract hard-to-find candidates.

Kaplan has the tools!

For students of every age, Kaplan offers the best-written, easiest-to-use books. Our growing library of titles includes guides for academic enrichment, test preparation, school selection, admissions, financial aid, and career and life skills.

Kaplan sets the standard for educational software with award-winning, innovative products for building study skills, preparing for entrance exams, choosing and paying for a school, pursuing a career, and more.

Helpful videos demystify college admissions and the SAT by leading the viewer on entertaining and irreverent "road trips" across America. Hitch a ride with Kaplan's Secrets to College Admission and Secrets to SAT Success.

Kaplan offers a variety of services online through sites on the Internet and America Online. Students can access information on achieving academic goals; testing, admissions, and financial aid; careers; fun contests and special promotions; live events; bulletin boards; links to helpful sites; and plenty of downloadable files, games, and software. Kaplan Online is the ultimate student resource.

EDUCATIONAL CENTERS

KAPLAN

Want more information about our services, products,
or the nearest Kaplan educational center?

---------------------------- HERE ----------------------------

Call our nationwide toll-free numbers:

1–800–KAP–TEST

(for information on our live courses, private tutoring and admissions consulting)

1–800–KAP–ITEM

(for information on our products)

1–888–KAP–LOAN*

(for information on student loans)

Connect with us in cyberspace:

On AOL, keyword "Kaplan"

On the Internet's World Wide Web, open "http://www.kaplan.com"

Via E-mail, "info@kaplan.com"

Write to:

Kaplan Educational Centers
888 Seventh Avenue
New York, NY 10106